A Handbook for Authentic Learning in Higher Education

An accessible resource to develop authentic learning and teaching in higher education, this book challenges conventional teaching practice and presents meaningful and impactful alternatives across disciplines that are research informed, student centred and achievable.

Bringing together a wide range of contemporary examples, this essential text shows how academics from an increasing range of disciplines and fields have shifted their attention away from the restrictions of campus-based education. Using engaging case study material, underpinned by cutting-edge research, the text shares innovations from over 50 different institutions, offers practical advice on how to facilitate authentic learning in real world contexts and examines the range of alternative assessment techniques available to the contemporary teacher.

A Handbook for Authentic Learning in Higher Education is ideal reading for early-career academics exploring approaches to learning, established academics searching for practical guides to emergent pedagogies and all those responsible for leading teaching and learning practices within their department or institution.

Andy Pitchford is Head of Learning and Teaching at the University of Bath, UK.

David Owen is a consultant and associate at the National Coordinating Centre for Public Engagement and the University of Bristol, UK.

Ed Stevens is Manager of the Arts & Humanities Research Institute at King's College, London, UK.

A Handbook for Authentic Learning in Higher Education

Transformational Learning Through
Real World Experiences

Andy Pitchford, David Owen
and Ed Stevens

Routledge
Taylor & Francis Group

LONDON AND NEW YORK

First published 2021
by Routledge
2 Park Square, Milton Park, Abingdon, Oxon OX14 4RN

and by Routledge
52 Vanderbilt Avenue, New York, NY 10017

Routledge is an imprint of the Taylor & Francis Group, an informa business

© 2021 Andy Pitchford, David Owen and Ed Stevens

British Library Cataloguing-in-Publication Data
A catalogue record for this book is available from the British Library

Library of Congress Cataloging-in-Publication Data
Names: Pitchford, Andy, author.
Title: A handbook for authentic learning in higher education : transformational learning through real world experiences / Andy Pitchford, David Owen, and Ed Stevens.
Description: Abingdon, Oxon ; New York, NY : Routledge, 2021. | Includes bibliographical references and index.
Identifiers: LCCN 2020019357 (print) | LCCN 2020019358 (ebook)
Subjects: LCSH: Transformative learning. | Student-centered learning. | College teaching—Methodology.
Classification: LCC LC1100 .P58 2021 (print) | LCC LC1100 (ebook) | DDC 378.1/25—dc23
LC record available at https://lccn.loc.gov/2020019357
LC ebook record available at https://lccn.loc.gov/2020019358

ISBN: 978-0-367-19723-0 (hbk)
ISBN: 978-0-367-19724-7 (pbk)
ISBN: 978-0-429-24285-4 (ebk)

Typeset in Sabon
by Apex CoVantage, LLC

Contents

Introduction

This book is about a particular way of organising learning in higher education. It's about opening up universities so that staff and students can learn from the world around them and make contributions that reflect their capacities and potential. It's founded on a series of ideas about higher education that the three of us share, having worked in a variety of roles within, beyond and between universities. We all have faith in the ability of universities to partner effectively with communities and external organisations and believe passionately in the civic mission of our institutions. We're all constructivists, in the sense that we regard students as being talents to unlock rather than vessels to fill, and we all lead or encourage innovation and creativity in our professional roles.

This alignment of values created the foundation for the work that has gone into the production of this handbook. However, in the early stages of writing, it soon became clear that we also shared a particular approach to team working, in the sense that in Belbin's (1993) description of team players, we were all 'plants', happily pondering new ideas and offering different perspectives while making little actual progress with the task at hand. This makes for stimulating conversation but is less helpful when it comes to action, and our lack of any 'completer-finisher' tendencies may be evident in the chapters that follow. We've done our best with the dots and crosses, and with the excellent support of our editors at Routledge, we hope that we've created a fluent and accessible text, but we're very confident that you'll discover some loose ends. We pose plenty of questions and don't answer them all, we point to some aspects of authentic learning work that are challenging and problematic, and we don't always provide solutions.

We hope, dear reader, that these unanswered questions represent a baton that you'll carry forward and, in their posing, that they provide you with pause for thought, a spur to critically reflect on your own practice of, or plans for, authentic learning. Our aim has been to celebrate and share the innovations of colleagues so that others may be inspired and so that those who wish to follow in their footsteps can do so with a knowledge of some of the shortcuts and some of the tripwires. We also hope that by showcasing the ingenuity of academic staff across a variety of disciplines and fields, and in a wide range of institutions, we demonstrate the value of these approaches so that they can be considered more widely and adopted with greater confidence.

Our focus for the handbook has been 'authentic learning.' We're well aware of the contested nature of the concept of authenticity more generally and are indebted to Carolin Kreber and the clarity offered by her seminal (2013) account of how the various interpretations of authenticity relate to higher education and to the lives of academics more broadly. However, we'll not labour over these distinctions, as our concern isn't – primarily at least – a spiritual quest, ethical exploration or political commentary. Instead, our interest is in what Kreber describes as the "perspective that suggests that what makes learning experiences authentic is that they are situated in, or correspond to, the 'real world' or appropriate social and disciplinary contexts" (2013: 11).

The kinds of learning experience that we pursue in the pages that follow are those that connect the capacities generated in higher education to concerns and communities beyond the campus walls. Such a connection lay at the outset of mediaeval universities, focused as they were in training religious, medical and legal elites and, in so doing, enhancing the economic development and status of a region (Martin, 2012). The turn to a more 'academic' education, one rooted in pure, objective knowledge, arose in European universities in the latter part of the C18th, driven by the works and ideals of Wihelm von Humboldt. Von Humboldt was a neo-humanist who championed the essential unity of teaching and research alongside "a high level of autonomy with professors and students free to seek truth and knowledge as they understood them" (ibid: 550).

Universities eagerly adopted von Humboldt's approach and so began a tradition of scholars in university settings resisting external influence and attempting to retain the purity and 'objectivity' of the knowledge that they generated. By distancing themselves from the profane, from mundane or everyday concerns, scholars have attempted to create learning and laboratory conditions that are protected from infection by pecuniary interest, from interference by the state or other sponsors. These attempts to foster academic 'freedom' – that is, the autonomy to pursue 'truth' – somewhat represent a 'golden age' discourse which, in a study of younger UK academics, Archer (2008a: 272) found to be "both desired and resisted as impossible, unfeasible and anachronistic – as epitomising an 'ivory tower' discourse of academia that is unsustainable within the present."

Yet there's no doubt that many scholars tend towards a more general distancing of universities from their host communities and economies. They also tend towards systems of instruction and assessment that are abstracted from settings or circumstances, that are predominantly theoretical but lack application. We don't seek to use this handbook to challenge notions of academic

freedom or the value of pure research. We do, however, want to draw attention to those forms of learning that are more connected, more engaged and
more applied. In our experience, they represent opportunities for students
to engage more fully with their discipline or subject, to feel a greater sense
of purpose and to sense their own agency – their ability to act in and on the
world, to shape it and to change it.

Authentic learning for us reflects those episodes where complex, 'higher'
knowledge comes to life through application. It's where learning is planned
and structured with the intention of enabling students, and staff, to deploy
their understanding and capabilities for the benefit of others. To achieve
this, learning experiences and journeys need to be organised in new and
different ways. The successful application of knowledge requires forms of
engineering and infrastructure that connect academic communities to the
places and spaces where this work will impact or be done. If we throw open
the doors and break out of the classroom, we'll need somewhere else to go,
people who will welcome us and purposeful activities to pursue. If the doors
remain open, we need to ensure that others who enter the classroom are
appropriately prepared, supported and rewarded.

Our interpretation of authentic learning owes much to the work of Fred
Newmann and Anthony Herrington, both of whom have inspired the delivery of new forms of learning within and beyond their own shores. Newmann et al. (2007), for example, characterise authentic learning as involving
originality in the construction of knowledge that produces value beyond the
school or university. It focuses on the production of solutions but always
on the basis of experiential rather than abstracted learning. The purpose is
to create mutual benefit for the student and for the recipient of the knowledge, not just for the 'bureaucracy' or the university machine. Herrington's
work, meanwhile (consider Herrington and Herrington, 2006; Herrington
and Oliver, 2000; Herrington and Herrington, 1998), points us towards key
components of authentic learning, including:

- Collaboration and interdisciplinarity
- Sensible, meaningful, immersive, engaging activities
- The pursuit of a single, complex task over an extended period of time
- The ability to learn from expert, model 'performances'
- Supportive coaching and scaffolding
- The use of reflection
- The production of useful, valued artefacts and outputs

For some time, our interest has been in how this kind of learning can be
achieved. It's one thing to value and desire greater application and engagement but quite another to work out precisely how to do it. This has become
our quest, to locate good practice in a range of fields and institutions and
to share the ways in which colleagues have brought these approaches to

life. We hope that this will be useful, not least because we're not alone in our interest in the field, and from our own networks, we're aware of many academic colleagues keen to understand how innovations have been created and how they might build on these forms of practice in their own institutions.

The apparent increase in attention to authentic learning can be attributed to a number of interrelated themes. There are some, for example, Boehm (2019), who feel that we're moving into a new phase of development in higher education that will encourage us to think more deeply about the nature of the experiences that we create – deliberately or accidentally – for learners. The increasing ubiquity of knowledge and the changing nature of access to higher education suggests to Boehm that we're moving away from the modes of delivery that focused on the transmission and, later, the curation of knowledge, towards a mode that is much more concerned with the ways in which students and scholars make sense of the many different influences on their understanding. Universities will, in this view, become places where the facilitation and construction of knowledge become more important that the acquisition of facts. In other words, universities will create pathways and experiences that enable learners to make sense of both academic and disciplinary knowledge and to understand how to apply this knowledge in different settings and environments. Universities will take responsibility for these interfaces, where societal or community needs meet bodies of disciplinary knowledge and where students have the opportunity to synthesise and create solutions. Higher education will become a series of experiences or journeys that enable students to learn most effectively about their discipline, the world around them and their potential contribution to both domains.

This vision also reflects the potential for authentic learning to engage students more effectively in their education. We operate in an era when students at all levels are perceived as increasingly alienated, distanced from the deeper purposes of their education and motivated largely by their desire to acquire credentials. The danger of such instrumentality is that it leads to students learning superficially and to an experience that is compartmentalised and focused on learning 'for the test.' Government policies and consumerism are held liable for these deep shifts, but authentic learning experiences are frequently seen as an antidote to this malaise, creating opportunities for students to take control, recognise and realise their potential and work in meaningful, accessible and relevant settings. Learning in 'real world' environments can help students to make sense of the knowledge that's presented to them, to develop a desire to learn more and to master the subject and to create a positive sense of purpose and accountability. It helps students move from bystander to actor, from lurker to contributor, from the periphery to the centre.

Other colleagues may have more pragmatic concerns. Traditional, lecture and examination-based delivery models tend not to support the development of the kinds of transferable skills demanded by C21st employers. However, experiential modes – where students are actively applying their knowledge and capacities – are seen as more conducive to employability. Authentic learning carries the possibility of students acquiring greater contextual understanding of the workplace or of the sector with which they're most closely associated. It also presents the possibility that students will create ideas and solutions that carry value in other markets; authentic learning can create conditions for innovation and enterprise that may not otherwise be easy to facilitate. Additionally, Sotiriadou et al. (2019) argue that authentic learning can counter tendencies towards cheating, partly because students become more intrinsically motivated in the activity at hand but also because the 'bespoke' or specialised nature of the learning activity mitigates against contract cheating and the provision of formulaic responses to standardised questions (see also Villarroel et al., 2018; James and Cassidy, 2018).

Finally, as we'll see in the chapters that follow, there are colleagues who are committed to bringing together the various missions of the university in order to promote new forms of collaboration and co-operation and to maximise the potential impact of the institution as a whole. This might entail finding greater synergy between the educative and research functions of the university or recognising how both of these realms might contribute to civic, public engagement or outreach activities. There are also colleagues who hope that by finding greater alignment between these separate functions, we might make more sense of the system of the university as a whole. For those of us who occasionally find aspects of academic life mildly absurd, whether we're lecturing to hundreds of disinterested faces or under pressure to write at length for exceptionally small audiences, authentic learning might bring some sense, clarity and optimism. This has been our experience, anyway, and we're keen to share the love.

The book itself is organised around two major areas of concern. First, through a series of chapters, we consider the general climate of higher education and its constituent institutions so that readers can contemplate how they might approach authentic learning activities and their development. We also consider some of the more fundamental 'how-to' questions. Second, we celebrate and share a series of case studies that demonstrate the many ways in which authentic learning can be managed and facilitated. The case studies themselves have been selected on the basis of criteria that we hope provide some clarity and consistency but also recognise the ways in which authentic learning is manifested in a very wide range of disciplines and fields and at institutions of all kinds up and down the country. Our criteria for case studies were:

1   The cases facilitated learning that reflected the definitions or authenticity offered by Herrington and Newmann (op cit).
2   The cases demonstrated innovation and ingenuity that enabled both undergraduate and postgraduate students to apply their disciplinary or subject knowledge in contexts beyond the traditional classroom, laboratory or studio.
3   The cases were from universities within the higher education system of the United Kingdom. We acknowledge the global development of authentic learning in Chapter 5 but have not presented any examples from the international context.
4   The interactions had to be real, in the sense that learning was applied to settings that existed independently of the university and not constructed with the sole purpose of facilitating the development of students or the advancement of the institution concerned. We ruled out a number of simulations on this basis.
5   The cases were part of the formal curriculum. We wanted to show that the approaches could be legitimately and usefully adopted as a central part of the student's learning journey rather than as a downgraded option in the extra or co-curricula realm.
6   The cases offered students agency and the ability to make an impact, leave an imprint upon or change the setting that they entered.
7   The cases created an artefact or resource that could contribute to the learning of others within or beyond the university, now or in the future.
8   The cases reflected diversity in terms of disciplines and fields of study and in terms of host institutions, whether teaching or research intensive.

By applying the criteria, we're able to share a range of approaches that create bridges or pathways from the activity of study to new settings for application. They're most easily understood as forms of infrastructure or learning architecture – they scaffold, support and guide the learner towards meaningful interaction and application. Some are necessarily based on partnerships with other internal and external agencies, and some are more focused on university resources and connections, although these are fewer in number.

The cases build on consultancy work that David carried out for the Centre for Learning & Teaching and the Public Engagement Unit at the University of Bath in 2017. At this point in time, the university was beginning a major programme of curriculum transformation and was searching for new ways to enliven teaching, engage its students and connect more meaningfully with external stakeholders. While David's work was immensely valuable for Bath, it was clear that the enormous variety of 'engaged' or authentic approaches that he had identified in UK institutions deserved a wider audience. We have, therefore, collectively extended David's original research to offer the range of case studies presented in this handbook. We're grateful to the University of Bath for helping to initiate the idea and for enabling us to acquire ethical approval for the research elements of the work undertaken.[1]

The book takes the following structure. In Chapter 1, we consider five key narratives that characterise contemporary Western higher education. These narratives can be both enabling and constraining, so we offer torchlight to help colleagues to see through some of the fog. We consider the virtues and nature of the 'ivory tower', debates over where to learn and how to learn, vocationalism and 'dumbing down', students and consumerism and the varying interpretations of university missions. Chapter 2 moves towards more practical considerations of how authentic learning can be positioned, designed and constructed. We consider how to engage with and respond to external influences and position these choices in relation to a range of pedagogical traditions before examining the components of an authentic curriculum and how the various pieces of the learning jigsaw can be aligned to create new and more effective experiences for the student. The chapter concludes with a consideration of the forms of assessment most suited to authentic learning. In Chapter 3, we assess the ways in which colleagues can form lasting and sustainable partnerships with external agencies and consider how partnerships can be mutually beneficial and non-exploitative. Chapter 4 explores how colleagues at different points in their career journeys can initiate, support or contribute to the kinds of change that would lead to the further proliferation of authentic learning. We consider how this kind of work differs from more traditional interpretations of academic life and how we all might offer support and collaboration to those seeking to embark on this journey. In Chapter 5, we look further afield to explore the ways in which authentic learning has evolved in other countries and offer inspiration from universities operating with radically different resources and in cultures that pose very different challenges for their higher education institutions. Our Conclusion pulls together some, if not all, of the threads to help us build a case for further experimentation and to encourage universities more generally to support those who take the decision to lead change, to improve learning and to innovate at a time when more bureaucratic, more formulaic responses may be the norm.

Sandwiched between these chapters, like the heady and intoxicating rollercoaster ride of a placement year, are the case studies. If nothing else, these cases are a tribute to colleagues up and down the country who have had the guts and imagination to create inspiring interventions. We thank them for sparing their valuable time to talk with us, for sharing their insights and explaining the history and detail of their particular methods. We hope they continue to overcome the hurdles that are placed before them and that their success is recognised and their contributions suitably valued.

Finally, we hope that you like what you read here and that you'll take confidence from the success of others to design your own authentic learning experiences, to work with students and other partners to have a positive impact on the world and to continue to work with the best interests of all stakeholders at heart.

Note

1 We carried out structured telephone interviews with key contacts at each institution in order to ensure that our interpretation of their approach was informed and accurate.

Chapter 1

Arguing for authentic learning

Introduction

The purpose of this chapter is to help those who wish to develop new approaches to teaching, particularly those who can see an opportunity to bring authenticity into their curriculum in the ways that we've characterised. We recognise that the process of change is challenging and complex and that institutional life is full of unexpected events, hurdles and barriers. Universities are wonderfully enabling environments, but they often contain structures that inhibit and constrain, intentionally or not. They also house individuals who, for all kinds of reasons, will ask difficult questions about the changes we wish to bring. Some of these questions are designed to help us refine our ideas and propositions; some of them are designed to block our progress. Our success, and our sanity, will be enhanced if we're able to spot the difference.

This chapter is therefore an introduction to some of the narratives and debates that surround attempts to innovate in higher education curricula. By fostering an understanding of these accounts, we hope to enable you to determine the following things:

1 How to generate support for teaching and learning proposals in the context of your institution.
2 The extent to which barriers or challenges are 'real' – we might even say authentic – or whether they're a mask for other objections, fears or insecurities.
3 Ways in which to protect and defend innovations at key stages of development.
4 How best to learn from all those involved in the process of teaching and learning design – those with experience, and those without.

This isn't a conventional 'theory' chapter. Although we're now pretty exhausted having written it, the chapter isn't remotely exhaustive in terms of the literature. We make reference to key texts and documents, but this is so that you have the chance to pursue arguments and debates in more detail. We substantiate our own positions where necessary, but our overall aim is to present debates and discussions with which we – and the many colleagues responsible for the success of our case studies – are intimately familiar. We know that you're likely to face these challenges at some stage of your journey towards innovation, so we offer some guidance through these occasionally choppy waters.

The chapter is organised around debates under five broad sections:

1   The virtues of the ivory tower
2   How to learn and where to learn
3   Vocationalism and dumbing down
4   Students and consumerism
5   Valuing diversity in higher education

In the sections that follow, we aim to characterise the kinds of questions that will be raised by friendly, or unfriendly, colleagues when the possibility for change arises. We also hope to pinpoint responses or contributions that will allow you to pick your way through these challenges and to keep faith with ideas that might otherwise be derailed or undermined.

The virtues of the ivory tower

There's a set of ideas about university teaching and learning that can be found in the corridors and offices of all universities. These ideas are not universally held, but in some places, depending on the discipline, the institution and the ages and demography of the individuals involved, they may dominate. Sometimes, this domination will be at the expense of other conceptions, and sometimes it will be an unspoken 'common-sense' communicated subtly by the raising of an eyebrow, a skyward look or a stifled laugh.

The ideas relate to the virtues of a university as an ivory tower, of a protected realm, unsullied by everyday concerns, in which truth can be pursued without fear of contradiction by external interests. Those who inhabit the tower do so with great legitimacy, given their intelligence, academic achievement and the respect that emanates from their peers. They're necessarily disconnected and separated from the practicalities of life as it's experienced by the majority of the population, in order that they'll be able to benefit from leisure, peace and calm rather than being constantly distracted by more worldly temptations. With these protections, knowledge can be pursued 'for its own sake', not in order to fulfil a contract or to satisfy some vested interest. Academics should, in this view, be free to pursue the knowledge and truths that they deem necessary to ensure the furtherance of their discipline or the insight for which they have responsibility. None of this should be subordinated to everyday concerns or to demands to engage more directly in the humdrum troubles of the locality. Academic freedom therefore protects the sanctity of scientific enquiry but can also be used as a defence against calls for the application of research or for wider collaboration (Martin, 2012).

To be a student in this version of a university is to acknowledge the wisdom of those who lay claim to valuable knowledge by virtue of their reading, searching or experimentation. These people have knowledge to profess, to declare publicly, and a student attends in order to share in this declaration. The implication is that those who are closest to the knowledge, who have the most nuanced and intimate understanding, are those best placed to explain it. Lectures, the traditional signifier of a distinctively higher education, make sense in this setting. Hear from the horse's mouth, learn from the experts, discover the knowledge at the cutting edge. The benefits of this approach have been evidenced throughout the centuries, from the original tiered lecture spaces at Padua and Bologna to the U-shaped adaptations at Harvard and other more contemporary institutions. Technology-rich lecture theatres now enhance the experience, which can be recorded and shared more widely and at a speed to ensure that all glean the required information. Seminars, tutorials and laboratories afford students the opportunity to test and clarify this knowledge, sharing understanding with peers, refining assumptions, receiving feedback.

Students typically join a university that comprises departments, schools, faculties or colleges that in turn reflect disciplines and fields of study. All of these organisations confer status and prestige and make these rewards clear to all by public pronouncements and through rituals, ceremonies, clothing and other awards and signs. Status is also communicated through titles and qualifications, many of which hark back to the ecclesiastical roots of many institutions. The result is a complicated web of hierarchies, expectations and relationships that's continually reproduced and which constantly attracts new members, keen to enjoy the benefits that they have seen from a distance as a student. People work very hard to enter these communities and harder still to succeed in them. The communities are prized because they have produced knowledge of unquestionable value and offer their members largely rewarding and respected lives that reflect long-held expectations. These are structures that have evolved over several centuries and imply wisdom, merit and achievement (see Barnett, 2014; Lea and Street, 2006).

We paint this picture because those of us who suggest new ways of working in this realm will often encounter hostility and recalcitrance, most frequently from those who represent this, the 'classical' interpretation of university life (see Martin, op cit). This is sometimes because more experienced colleagues will wish to critique new ideas in the hope that they'll become more refined and more likely to enjoy success. It is also, however, because new ways of working imply a threat to the status quo and to the structures that support the status of those who have been successful on the basis of this established understanding or whose expectations of university life are grounded only in these conventional ideas. It's of course true that this view of university life has some value, and few of us are likely to suggest that scientific enquiry should be curtailed in some way or universities made more subject to the demands of the state or the market. However, the traditional view of university life also conflates several rather questionable notions and tends to lament a 'golden age' of university life and enquiry, when the good work of a university went unquestioned, when academic freedom was protected and respected by all and when academics could enjoy an unencumbered view from the ivory tower to pursue their work without hindrance.

Identifying the specific period that's characterised by the 'golden age' can prove challenging. Thody (2012) shows how the growth of British universities in the past 200 years has been marked by considerable diversity, not simple reproduction of an existing or dominant form. There has been no great period of stability, and no unifying view of the purpose of universities in this time. As we'll see, many institutions developed in architectural isolation from their locales, but no institution has, to our knowledge, ever succeeded in building an actual ivory tower. Shapin (2012) demonstrates that this Biblical figure of speech only became associated with universities in the 1930s. It has been used in both a positive and a disparaging sense to describe the disengagement of artists, scientists and intellectuals from everyday life, but it doesn't accurately describe any buildings, past or present, at Oxford or Cambridge or other British universities. Conflating ideas around Oxbridge colleges and ivory towers helps to enforce conventional views about the nature of university life but masks the complex histories of those institutions, which have at various times worked intimately with external organisations and communities in order to develop knowledge and educate students. There have never been any physical ivory towers, and the metaphorical ones have only been inhabited occasionally, by particular disciplines and fields of study at particular stages of development.

Understanding the contested and constructed nature of university life can help us to recognise that while particular conceptions of study and learning may dominate, many others are possible. While some colleagues seek to valorise a traditional or conventional view of how we ought to act as academics, other possibilities are evident in the histories of universities and in the logical extension of their missions or core values.

How to learn and where to learn

When considering what it is that makes a university experience distinctive from, say, a school or the workplace, the ideas of the lecture and the campus continue to dominate. The lecture is still seen as the characteristic mode of learning in higher education, and the campus marks the boundary of this community, a physical space designed for particular forms of learning, controlled and surveyed in order to guarantee the quality of the education. Unpacking the history of both of these notions can help us to challenge conventional wisdom while still appreciating the insight of those who have contributed to the development of these forms in the first place.

The lecture is a form of one-to-many verbal communication. Its history is intertwined with other related practices in religious and political settings, including the sermon and the speech. It's centred on the sharing of knowledge by an individual who holds a monopoly position, either to the ownership of the knowledge in question or to its analysis. Given that lecturing emerged as a practice in advance of the advent of the printing press, it's also possible to associate it with the art of town crying. Curiously, of all of these practices, only lecturing appears to be in what we might describe a growth position, all of the others having been undermined by the arrival of new technologies. The resilience of lecturing as a practice could be explained, in principle, due to the need for academics to preserve an activity that affords them status and makes clear who holds authority – in all senses. It could also be explained by its unique effectiveness and by the ways in which the lecture has been refined over time in order to maximise student learning.

In order for the latter point to hold, we would need to find evidence of significant advances in practice over time. This is not easy to do, as beyond the application of presentation packages and more recently the use of recording and distribution software, the practice of lecturing is essentially the same as it's always been, in that a single person, who is uniquely skilled or informed, shares their knowledge in a verbal format. There is, on the contrary, much evidence to suggest that as an educative form, the lecture is deeply problematic (Freeman et al., 2014; Bligh, 2000; Gibbs, 1981). We don't want to suggest that a lecture can't be inspirational, because we have all borne witness to great oratory or been engaged effectively by a well-organised class, but we do want to argue that it's simply one form amongst many and that its apparent domination may be due to historical factors rather than any great advances over time or evidence that proves its worth. Other forms of teaching and learning may be more effective and should not be discouraged.

The notion of the campus is, meanwhile, tied to ideas about residential education and intentional communities. In the United Kingdom, we assume that the ideal higher education is necessarily residential, that it makes sense to travel to a new setting for the benefits and rites of passage that accrue. We know, however, that this approach isn't shared in many other countries, and indeed historically in the United Kingdom, the principle hasn't been consistently applied. While monastic life and ecclesiastical education have relied on the development of communities separated from everyday life, this distancing wasn't a feature of the ancient incarnations of universities in Europe. Rather, Klinenberg (2018) argues, the enclosed quadrangles of Oxford were a gradual response to tensions between Town and Gown, and while the students required protection, the architecture also afforded the college authorities greater surveillance of their charges and greater control over their behaviour.

Most of these early universities grew in urban environments, and while they gradually created exclusive spaces for their students, these spaces were largely integrated into their host cities rather than being an entirely separate settlement. The idea of the campus was largely an American invention, owing much to the availability of cheap land on the outskirts of cities (Turner, 1987). The American conception of the campus incorporated residential life and made a virtue of interdisciplinarity and informal learning. In turn, this idea inspired the growth and design of new institutions in the United Kingdom and beyond in the C20th, with many modelling their provision on the out-of-town campus model. As a result, we can now see a range of approaches to place and space in British universities, with some institutions inhabiting and, in some cases, dominating their host towns and cities and with others set apart, on a green or brownfield site or on top of a windy hill with the city in the distance.

Although British universities have, over the centuries, become distinctive places, separated in various ways from their host communities, this process has long had its critics. While many have seen this distancing as a virtue, others have expressed concern about the superiority implied by separation and of the failure of institutions to prepare students for citizenship and with an awareness of the circumstances of those less fortunate than themselves. Universities have been responding to these criticisms for over two centuries, with the mission and settlement movements at Oxford and Cambridge in the C19th the most obvious demonstration of the desire to help students understand more about their social circumstances and to instil a desire to reach beyond the campus environment and to work with more deprived communities (see Brewis, 2014). Since then, universities have in various ways sought to break down the real or imagined walls that prevent greater understanding on both sides, through outreach, widening participation initiatives, public and community engagement and more recently a desire for universities to become anchor institutions for local economies or to understand more fully their roles as part of the civic infrastructure.

In recent years, opportunities associated with mass higher education and more liberal markets have led to many questioning the need for a campus as it's conventionally understood. This notion can be tracked back to the founding of the Open University in 1969 but now extends to institutions which are almost entirely virtual (consider Arden University), are reliant on borrowed accommodation in cities across the world (for example, Minerva – www.minerva.kgi.edu), those who simply rent iconic buildings (for example, the University Campus of Football Business, UFBC, based at Wembley and Etihad Stadiums) or which are located in business settings on the basis of strategic partnerships. Increasingly, British universities are engaging more deeply with local authorities in order to secure planning consent for capital development or are developing partnerships with those organisations in order to create new spaces that have both civic and educational purposes (for example, The Hive library in Worcester, the Sport Dock at East London or Imperial's White City Campus). All of these developments demonstrate fluidity, new ways to approach and understand educational spaces, new ways for universities to engage with place.

Vocationalism and dumbing down

The idealised vision of a university offers academics freedom from interference and the opportunity to discover and construct knowledge in a way that is unhindered by external influences. As a result, contract research always carries with it the threat of constraint or subordination. Status accrues from the ability to secure significant external funds for research or enterprise, but a shadow of doubt remains because another piper is calling the tune. Is this work in the pursuit of truth or the pursuit of profit? Scepticism also abounds when degree courses are associated with particular occupations or professions, as students will be occupied not in the quest for knowledge but in a quest for compliance and docility, with the ultimate aim of submitting their will and personality sufficiently so that they can become dutiful employees.

While this scepticism harks back to our mythical 'golden age', it also overlooks the fact that higher education has always been closely aligned to preparation for particular forms of work. To accuse a course or programme of being 'vocational' often implies a lack of intellectual challenge, unworthy of university enterprise or approval. But the reality is that from their very inception, universities have been training their students for work in the church, in education and in those professional areas deemed legitimate, or of sufficient status, at any point in time (Boud and Solomon, 2001). Medicine and law, disciplines that remain unquestioned when it comes to their 'higher' credentials, are explicitly vocational. They develop both knowledge and skills that are appropriate to their profession. We might even go one stage further and argue that the most established or traditional disciplines, mathematics and philosophy, for example, are organised in order to create a new generation of mathematicians and philosophers, trained in the rigours of those fields, ready to extend the legacy of those who worked so hard to establish the field in the first place (Becher and Trowler, 2001).

To a great extent, these implied criticisms of applied learning, and of linking study to external concerns and priorities, are hollow. They do, however, mask confusion over those capacities with which higher education should be concerned. Lurking in the background is the assumption that the cultivation of the mind and the acquisition of knowledge are the primary aims of a university education. Skills, in contrast, are of lesser importance, and a higher education is devalued if these faculties acquire too much prominence. This, in turn, obscures the fact that a university education has always been about the development of both knowledge and skills. Millican and Bourner (2014) show how this dominant view reflected the idea that a degree should ensure the possession of knowledge but also the ability to think critically. This skill would help to ensure the future employability of students, and support the continued progress of the discipline or field. Other core skills in reading, listening, reflecting and writing were essential elements of this approach. This view has come under attack in the past 30 years as our understanding of effective teaching and learning has become more advanced but also as greater recognition has emerged of the different forms of knowledge that may be appropriate in higher education and the wider range of skills that can be recognised and developed within the university curriculum.

It's also the case that the fields and disciplines themselves emphasise different forms and modes of learning. A typical degree in law will, for example, have rules at the centre and so is largely focused on the retention of facts and cases, aligned to a skill set attuned to the needs of a court room. The study of economics will encourage students to abstract ideas or models from the immediate context or to apply abstract models to new data or situations. Drama students will read and analyse and will be assessed on their acting performance; sports students will read and analyse and experiment but never be assessed on their sporting performance. Mathematicians learn languages, apply them and use tool kits to solve problems.

All disciplines and fields claim to develop knowledge and understanding, but they'll do this in many different ways. They also emphasise different forms of intelligence: some prioritise linguistic, others logic or existential or musical or kinaesthetic. The point is that academic subjects have been constructed in many different ways. They all have to carry legitimacy, so they have to be accepted by their key stakeholders in order to be respected and resourced. British higher education is actually a very broad church, encompassing all kinds of knowledge forms and capabilities. Even within a single institution, there will be huge variations in the ways in which capabilities are developed and assessed. This variety is often overlooked, and as a result, there will be some toleration of those who suggest that other subjects are lesser in some way, that some fields are more suited to higher education and that an emphasis on skills and vocationalism represents a dereliction of our duty as university educators. Instead, we want to argue that this great variety presents us with a range of opportunities. Rather than deride the 'other', rather than seek to advance our own status by denigrating the work of colleagues in different fields, we argue that we should embrace this diversity and seek to learn from the many different approaches that are evident across the sector today.

We do, of course, recognise that there has to be some criteria against which we can assess the 'higher' nature of the capabilities of concern here.

We understand that learning in a university has to be distinctive and more challenging than secondary or other forms of tertiary education. For us, the key to this is the extent to which university learning is, to echo McLean et al. (2018), transformative for the individual – does it make strong connections between the field of study and their own life experience? While university learning has to stretch us and take us into new domains and paradigms, it should also enable us imagine new approaches and solutions. It should therefore be open and creative but also cognisant of Barnett's (2011, 2014) reflections on the nature of will and of wisdom. Barnett has long argued for a recognition that knowledge and skills are insufficient as an explanation of what a university education does. In addition, he argues, we should consider the dispositions of students and the extent to which they have the desire to apply their learning to their lives, in the workplace and beyond. If it's possible to inculcate that desire to act and to share their knowledge with others, the next consideration is the extent to which they have the wisdom to know when and how to apply these capabilities. While the nature of the challenge in higher education is important to us, so too is the extent to which students have agency and can act – creatively and imaginatively – with the knowledge and skills that their disciplines have worked so hard to refine.

Students and consumerism

The huge changes that swept across UK higher education in the decades since 1992 have inevitably affected the ways in which students are perceived by those responsible for their education. Where once the motivations were simple, now they are complex. In the 'golden age', students progressed to higher education because they demonstrated the right qualities and were appropriate apprentices for the elite. They came with intrinsic motivation, ready to study a subject that they loved and respected. The grant system gave them the security they needed in order to explore and push the boundaries of their subject. Students in this world knew their place. They respected their discipline, appreciated the learning of their elders and understood the benefits of a higher education. They were the recipients of learning, who patiently took notes in order to capture the wisdom and insight of their tutors. They recognised the meritocracy and appreciated their position within it.

Today, all this has changed. The massive increase in numbers and institutions has, it's argued, had a deleterious effect on the quality of students. The fees regime has intensified instrumental approaches, so fewer students now have any sense of a love of their subject and are instead focused entirely on grades and their outcome. Worse still, the market exchange at the heart of the relationship has forced students to reconsider their role and identity. They now regard themselves primarily as consumers, with attendant rights and expectations, and their view of the role and position of their tutors has changed as a result (Naidoo et al., 2011; Naidoo and Jamieson, 2005). All of this is aggravated by the incursion of other market forces into higher education, particularly satisfaction indices (the National Student Survey or Graduate Outcomes Survey, for example) and audit or assessment frameworks (like the Teaching Excellence Framework) that force comparisons between institutions. Universities are now more managed than they ever have been before, academics are busier and more subservient and have less freedom and students have a misguided view of their position in the world and their ability to be successful within it (Tomlinson, 2017; Naidoo and Williams, 2015).

We do not seek to question many aspects of this view. Universities are undoubtedly organised very differently today, and new forms of management have long since taken hold (Deem et al., 2007). New segments of the population are entering the academy, and they bring with them new expectations and motivations. Many students today struggle with their experience in this system, and their apparent alienation, stress and anxiety is evident in many ways. Academic staff also struggle with shifting identities and the additional burdens that may accrue for some individuals with pastoral responsibilities. However, we don't think that the solution to these problems is to lament an age – however fictitious – when only an advantaged minority was able to access higher education, nor a time when the voice of students in the curriculum was so constrained and their ability to act so limited. Conceptualising the new relationships between universities and students in terms of consumption is one way to understand a different order, but others may be possible, too. Notions of membership or of mutuality may be helpful here. While the monetary exchange at the heart of the system can be interpreted as commercial or contractual, it could also be understood as payment for access to a community, for membership rights rather than consumer expectations (consider Crawford, 2012; Streeting and Wise, 2009).

Taking this approach might help us to think more about the power dynamics that characterise the relationship between universities, academic staff and students, particularly in relation to the curriculum. As Mann (2008) has argued, student wellbeing is served most effectively where there is encouragement to be active and to participate, to sense a contribution to a learning community. In contrast, the notion of students being part of an audience, deferring to expertise and authority, suggests an inert, subservient or sedentary existence. These considerations reflect what's known broadly as a constructivist approach to knowledge and learning. In this view, students shouldn't be regarded as mere recipients of information and interpretation, and if they're treated in this way, they'll tend towards a superficial mode of learning. Instead, their contribution to effective learning should be acknowledged, in the sense that all understanding builds upon previous experiences and interactions. It also relates to psychological factors, so confidence, belonging and identity all impact meaning and understanding. Constructivist approaches enhance the agency of the student; they tend towards activity and experience and the intersection of abstract theory with practical application and the realities of everyday life. Most, if not all, of the case studies that we present in this handbook are based on these same assumptions – that giving students a stake in their learning, and enabling them to apply their knowledge to meaningful situations, will pay dividends for their understanding and for their wellbeing (Healey et al., 2014; Mann, 2008).

Of course, in order to empower students, there has to be a concomitant release of power by those who held it previously. To make this work, academics have to reposition themselves and to work differently, to enable and facilitate rather than deliver. This may not be a popular course of action and may be a source of scepticism or opposition. However, we think that the benefits are significant. Adopting these approaches may not solve all of the problems of commodified education, but they will create space for students to make active contributions to their subject communities, to feel part of a greater project and to sense purpose and identity.

Valuing diversity in higher education

A great deal of condescension and pretension in higher education is caused by confusion over the fundamental purpose of the university. Prestige is afforded to some but not to others; certain capabilities are lauded and others disparaged for reasons that may make little sense to the external or neutral observer. Many will claim their expertise as the primary purpose of higher education or the one which should receive the most respect, resource or remuneration. In order to understand the potential roles that an institution can fulfil, we suggest that there are four dimensions to consider. In simple terms, these dimensions are 1) the function, so what does the university claim to do? 2) whom does it serve and how are these stakeholders positioned, so what are its markets and constituencies? 3) who can be seen to own the university, so who calls the shots? And 4) what's the context, so how is it affected by politics, economics and the environment?

Historically, there have been three broad missions – purposes stated in the constitution or articles of association or more recently the strategic plan. These relate firstly to knowledge, originally its storage, curation and interpretation but latterly its generation and validation, and so to research. Second, to the sharing of this knowledge in a way that enables individuals to grow and to pursue particular vocations, broadly understood, so to seek a career as an academic or in a realm associated with higher learning. This sharing can take the form of education, in the sense of the formulation of personality and character, or training, as in the direct preparation for work, to borrow Delanty's (2001) distinction. Third, universities have long had a public or intellectual role, where our most informed and respected experts bring their knowledge and wisdom to bear on the world beyond the campus walls. This may take the form of the communication of knowledge and research to wider publics or the engagement of academics in political, social or scientific debate.

Over time, emphasis on these different missions has shifted. It's possible to conceive of a university that focuses entirely on one of these realms and also to imagine one that balances efforts between the three. Where an institution has more than one focus, it's possible that competition will ensue between the champions of these different approaches. Each, however, has its own legitimacy. The predominance of one or another function will have little to do with any innate superiority or validity and more to do with the historic legacy of a particular institution or the contextual or political factors that enable its continued existence. It's difficult to consider ownership as a variable here, as we might do if we were seeking to explain the strategy or culture of a business organisation, because most UK universities are charities rather than being privately owned. However, it might instead be helpful to consider sponsors as an influencing factor. If, historically, the church was the first agency to fund and confer legitimacy upon the university, we can understand much of the early work of the institution in this context. In the centuries since the Middle Ages, central and local state have been the major donors in the United Kingdom, either directly through funding in various forms or through the regulation of the economy broadly or the higher education market specifically. We might consider concerns over private or commercial donations to universities a contemporary phenomenon, but in reality, universities have been seeking financial support from a wide range of individuals and organisations for centuries.

In most instances, the motives of a sponsor will be overt and straightforward. A philanthropic donor may wish others to benefit from the kind of education that they were able to enjoy; a commercial funder will have requirements for the furthering of particular forms of knowledge. The needs of other sponsors may be more complex, and there may not be the same desire to broadcast their intentions. This is particularly true in the case of the state, which on the surface may claim to wish to educate its citizenry in order to enrich cultural and economic life but which has, at various stages, been accused of expanding higher education in order to manage the challenges of youth unemployment and of influencing universities in order to ensure the propagation of values which support the status quo.

In the period since the Second World War, the state has overseen the transformation of higher education in the United Kingdom from a service offered to a privileged elite to an experience that's shared much more widely. This has involved the creation of new institutions, the introduction of new and separate funding regimes for research and teaching, new regulatory frameworks and a range of market interventions. This has affected not only who has been able to access higher education but how that education has been delivered. The introduction of polytechnics in the period after the Robbins Report in 1963 marked a period in which the educative function of institutions was given more consideration, with academics working in closer proximity to new sectors of the economy and demonstrating a willingness to embrace new approaches to learning. However, this process in turn created tensions within the educative function itself, with some arguing that the training requirements of external bodies were prioritised at the expense of character or personality formation. These concerns continue today and, since the Dearing Report (1997), have most frequently been voiced in the humanities and social sciences (see Collini, 2012; McLean, 2006). Those who seek to protect the moral purpose of a higher education, and its ability to inculcate capabilities which help to form better citizens, see danger in any attempt to tie learning to the narrow requirements of a particular workplace or profession. These fears are compounded where students are perceived as exhibiting instrumental motivations, learning to the test and exhibiting characteristics of the consumer.

The continued expansion of the university sector since the turn of the century has led to increasing calls for the academy to be 'accountable' in various ways. The state forces accountability to the market through attempts to force and expose competition, and as students enter into new contractual arrangements, they too call institutions and individuals to order. The state also expects universities to explain and take responsibility for the contribution that their research makes to society, economy and the environment and to ensure that the benefits of this are articulated through the Research Excellence Framework (REF). The need to ensure impact leads in turn to a consideration of the extent to which academic knowledge reaches different segments of the population and economy, and so in turn, public engagement has become a consideration for universities. More recently, the local state – itself under threat – has intensified calls for universities to reconsider their role in local communities and economies, and so civic engagement has become a realm where institutions are again being encouraged to take responsibility and account for their actions.

While these strategic imperatives reflect the need for universities to understand and respond to the needs of their sponsors, there's also pressure that accrues from the democratisation of higher education. By opening their doors to students from a wider range of backgrounds, universities become open to new demands, reflecting the experiences of different communities and stakeholder groups. From a social justice perspective, this is clearly to be welcomed and contributes to broader attempts to boost social mobility and equalise life chances, but for some within universities, this could be seen as further imposition and incursion and another burden to be avoided.

Universities in the United Kingdom are wonderfully diverse. Their variety demonstrates the strength of the sector and the ways in which institutions have built on their historic foundations. We have research-intensives, teaching-intensives, institutions that focus on the needs of their immediate communities or particular industrial interests and institutions that attempt to work across all of these areas. There is, we argue, no one mission or purpose that should be seen as primary or granted any elevated status. Universities vary in history, legacy, funding, location, culture and sponsor – they all bring something different to the party – but the pressures of accountability and competition are common to all. In the chapters that follow, we hope to demonstrate that with this variety comes great opportunity and that authentic learning offers the possibility of combining these missions and work areas in ways that create healthy efficiencies and collaborations. At the same time, it can build experiences for students that are inspiring and transformational.

Conclusion

In this chapter, we have considered five key narratives about learning and higher education. Our experience has shown us that these narratives are present, overtly or covertly, at a wide range of universities and that their presence is an inhibitor to change and enterprise. The narratives will sometimes undermine the confidence of those looking to innovate and at other times will be drawn upon directly in order to block or undermine an idea or intervention. While the narratives all have some basis in history and experience, elements of each are imagined or constructed, often in order to suit the situation of the author. Our intention has been to deconstruct and demythologise each of them, to enable you to respond appropriately when the need arises.

We hope that this wider understanding will help colleagues to maintain a critical perspective and help to support the confidence of those who can see that there's much to be gained from learning in new spaces and places, from working with new partners, from giving students greater agency and control over their learning and from enabling them to apply their knowledge and skills in settings beyond the classroom.

Chapter 2

Organising authentic learning

Introduction

This chapter will examine how authentic learning experiences can be created in order to enable students to learn effectively, understand and reflect upon their contributions and be appropriately supported and assessed. While we recognise the many challenges facing academics in the increasingly pressurised higher education environment, we aim for this to be a hopeful and optimistic chapter that demonstrates the many opportunities that exist to innovate and collaborate with partners within and beyond the university. We may live in difficult and occasionally dark times, but we believe that universities still afford us shafts of light where we can find the time and space to create new and inspiring approaches to education.

This chapter is designed to help develop understanding of the component elements of student learning in higher education and how these can be regarded as pieces of a jigsaw that can be used to build quite different pictures and landscapes. We hope that this will enable you to determine:

1 How to integrate elements of the student experience in order to create meaningful opportunities to develop authentic learning.
2 The ways in which such an approach might differ from more established approaches to the management of learning.
3 The forms of knowledge, skill and capability that can be developed in these contexts.
4 How these educational capacities can be informed, monitored and assessed.
5 How to align these elements in order to create a coherent approach to the management of learning episodes.

By highlighting the educational traditions which inform many of the cases that we present later in the handbook, we also offer you the opportunity to further explore the conceptual foundations of these approaches. The chapter is therefore structured around the following:

1 Classical approaches to the organisation of higher learning
2 Responding to the external environment
3 Pedagogical responses to new opportunities
4 Components of the curriculum and the potential for re-design
5 Knowledge, skills, action and assessment

In each of the sections that follow, we offer insights so that you may consider alternative ways to approach and organise learning. By presenting these options, we hope to stimulate your imagination to conceive of authentic learning experiences that promote the acquisition and development of higher order capabilities whilst simultaneously engaging with other aspects of your university's mission and enterprise.

Classical approaches to the organisation of higher learning

The classical approach to higher education, which we characterised in Chapter 1, tends to present the dissemination and acquisition of higher capacities as a straightforward process. This view is underpinned by dualist assumptions, with distinctions made between those with authority and those without, between scholars and students, between the lecturer and their audience and between those who are able and ready to produce knowledge and those whose role is simply to consume it.

The basic mode of learning reflects the ways in which the dominant disciplines and fields of study have developed in the United Kingdom over the past 300 to 400 years. Essentially, scientific understanding has been advanced by scholarship, the central tenet of which is critical thinking. Expertise has been refined gradually, and occasionally radically, by a process in which a community of peers commits arguments to scrutiny, seeking validation for any given premise, demanding substantiation for assertions, requiring logic and rationality. Given the need for the disciplines to grow, and to ensure a pipeline of future scholars and scientists, the emphasis on critical thinking is unsurprising. Students who gain expertise in their chosen realm, and who develop the core skills of argument construction and substantiation, are likely to serve their disciplines well. In addition, critical thinking is a transferable skill; it empowers graduates in a variety of settings, in the workplace and beyond. The education that has for so long suited the academy for its own purposes also carries value for other stakeholders. Disciplines and fields of study reproduce, and they do so in ways that tend to reflect the dominant people and ideas in those areas. In this way, it's possible to explain how the traditional narrative of higher education has developed, demanding independence whilst promoting the core values of criticality, rigour and review. The education that developed in this environment was one with a simple premise: that students should receive knowledge transmitted by experts and refine their understanding by learning and deploying the core skills of scholarship (see Barnett, 1997; Becher and Trowler, 2001).

As Millican and Bourner (2014) demonstrate, this narrative dominated interpretations of United Kingdom university life up until the 1980s. From this point onwards, confidence in the traditional view began to fracture. There were a number of reasons for this. On the domestic front, rising graduate unemployment raised questions about the suitability of the conventional approach. These concerns were exacerbated by the early moves towards mass higher education and the growth of the polytechnic and college sectors. If the country was producing more graduates, funded from the public purse, then greater attention was required to ensure that their education was fit for purpose, making meaningful contributions to the careers of individuals and to satisfying the needs of employing organisations. It was in this context that the transferable skills movement developed, with various people arguing that higher education had to offer more than merely an academic apprenticeship.

The continued growth of higher education through the 1990s was matched by a diversification in the range of subjects, with new relationships formed between universities and external organisations and new forms of knowledge and skill contemplated as part of the curriculum. At the same time, scholarship became infused with influences from across the globe. The critical lens that was employed in the service of disciplines was turned on academia itself, with consideration now given to how and why learning was delivered in particular ways, how individuals and communities might best learn in the future and how the exercise of power affected the potential of the educative enterprise. The emphasis shifted away from disciplines, colleges and faculties as the dominant parties in the relationship, towards the centralised functions of the university and – arguably – towards the satisfaction of the needs of students, as individuals and as communities.

Central to the many critiques of the traditional approach was that a narrow focus on the delivery of content and an implicit emphasis on the development of critical thinking are insufficient to guarantee the cognitive advance of individuals and the development of citizens or workers with appropriate capabilities for the C21st. Learners who lack a sense of purpose, confidence or identity are, for example, unlikely to prosper (consider Lizzio and Wilson, 2013) as scholars. Students who feel isolated, alienated or disengaged are unlikely to fulfil their potential in relation to their discipline, subject or vocation (see Mann, 2008). Graduates who aren't willing to utilise their capabilities to better themselves or their communities, or who lack the determination to overcome adversity, won't make the contributions to the wider world that they could or should do (see Barnett, 2013, 2014).

These challenges to the core business of the university are significant in their own right, but are largely the outcome of scholars questioning the internal mechanics of their educational institutions. To these views we can add the cacophony of voices from beyond the academy, whose volume has increased alongside the continued growth of the sector, who have called for a refocusing or realignment of curricula and teaching that would enable their interests to be better represented and reflected. It's to these external voices that our attention now turns.

Responding to the external environment

We noted in our first chapter the historic tendency for universities to adapt their business and approach in order to attend to the needs of their sponsors. This situation persists today, although the role of the state as the central actor in United Kingdom higher education has shifted in a way that mirrors fundamental changes in the forms of government that became prevalent in the late C20th. This reflects the dominance of particular ideological and policy orientations, with governments moving from a position of being the single central funding agency in the early period of growth in the 1990s to the situation where sponsors are more diversified, with the state operating in a facilitating capacity rather than as the major provider or regulator. The consequence of this is that the voices of other sponsors are moving centre stage, with those representing business interests most obviously in starring roles but with students and communities sharing at least some of the limelight.

These voices may emanate from individual organisations with research and development departments or may reflect the insight of particularly experienced individuals. They'll be articulated by policy agencies (for example, the World Economic Forum, 2018) or by representative bodies (consider the Institute of Student Employers, 2018), and while the emphasis within reports and presentations will reflect the particular need of the host organisation or sector, the basic message will be the same. Content and subject expertise remains important, but the claims of universities to monopoly and distinctiveness in this realm are weaker. Modern technologies make content ubiquitous, and universities increasingly struggle to convince the wider world that they should restrict access to the knowledge that they do generate or construct. Instead, external stakeholders call for greater emphasis on capabilities that have relevance beyond academia and that support independent learning in the long term and across the life-course.

Of course, many in universities will be suspicious of any attempt by big corporations to exert undue influence on education. There's the danger that a focus on employability will dilute or diminish attempts to prepare individuals to have independence of mind, democratic maturity and the ability to discern truth from bluster or propaganda. But in our experience, the reality of this discourse is more subtle, nuanced and complex than this view suggests. Some employers are, quite clearly, not in the business of promoting a radical critique of the established social order, but others continue to be interested in how education will respond to the increasing influence of mechanisation and artificial intelligence, how they might further develop corporate social responsibilities or their relationships with local communities and how their workplaces might become more diverse and inclusive. We don't intend to argue, in any way, that all's well with the state of late capitalism in C21st Britain but rather that the complexity and diversity of external demands on university curricula actually help us to negotiate a wide range of solutions. There is, in our view, still room to create interesting, innovative and empowering responses to these challenges. All is not lost.

The world of learning beyond content and subject expertise is articulated in a number of different ways. The notion of transferable skills has been widespread since the 1990s and refers to the potential of skills that are deliberately or accidentally developed within the curriculum to have relevance to a wide range of other settings. Typically, transferable skills will include elements of communication, teamwork, leadership, dependability, reliability and the capabilities associated with independent learning. Transferable skills are also often associated with analysis, problem solving and decision-making. In the late 1990s, a narrative developed around these capabilities, based on the work of Gibbons et al. (1994), which suggested a gradual shift in the way that knowledge was being produced and the skills that were implicitly required to participate in its construction. Crudely, this move was away from 'Mode 1' knowledge, characterised by established disciplines operating within the academy, towards 'Mode 2' knowledge, which was much more the outcome of inter- or multidisciplinary collaboration beyond the campus walls, judged by stakeholders other than academic peer communities. Although this work isn't without its critics (for example, Delanty, 2001), it has undoubtedly contributed to increasing consideration of the way in which a university education balances the acquisition of knowledge with its application and continued production. This begs questions of the extent to which university learning prioritises the upper echelons of Bloom's (1956) taxonomy or succumbs to more superficial, regurgitating or reproductive tendencies.

The diversification of fields of study since the early 1990s has enabled consideration within the academy of other ways of knowing, learning and developing. Design thinking, for example, which aims to create positive environments for the solution of complex or wicked problems, has been prevalent in a range of industry sectors since the 1970s (see Cross, 2011) but has only recently gained a foothold in academia. Systems thinking has a longer history in some university environments but still remains a peripheral body of knowledge and is also essentially inter- or multidisciplinary. It seeks to discern the 'whole system' in any setting and to develop understanding of the purpose of any component elements and how they align with the overall aim. Systems thinking is associated with lateral and strategic thinking, both of which lay claim to being separate and legitimate bodies of knowledge themselves (consider de Bono, 1992, 2015; Edmonson, 2018). Representatives of artistic or cultural interests will point to the need for greater emphasis on creative capacities in higher education curricula, as will those who argue that continued economic growth is predicated upon enterprise and innovation. This narrative will often extend to include consideration of Dweck's (2006) work on fixed and growth mindsets and the need to promote an outlook with a positive view of human agency and free will.

There are many forms of knowing and understanding that universities have been reluctant to embrace. Some of these have been overlooked for good reason, others in order to protect the status of those in positions of power within the disciplines. The increasing diversification of higher education, and the amplification of the voices of those outside the academy who have previously been ignored or side-lined, affords us the opportunity to think more imaginatively about what might be included in a course or programme and how it might be delivered. Alternative approaches may offer us more effective ways in which to develop the kinds of capacities and dispositions that graduates will need to face the increasingly complex, changing and ambiguous world that they will inhabit in the future (see Barnett, 2014).

Pedagogical responses to new opportunities

In all of our case studies, we share an aspiration to make a contribution to new interpretations of higher education. These interpretations encourage collaboration, either with other students, with staff at various levels or with other stakeholders within and beyond the campus. They also emphasise the value of experience and seek to structure the agency and activity of students in ways which facilitate the development of new and different capabilities. They ensure that students engage meaningfully with knowledge and do so in ways that acknowledge the contributions that all participants can make to the process. Despite these similarities, the cases are informed by different underlying assumptions, which in turn reflect broader pedagogical traditions.

Before considering more contemporary interpretations, it should be noted that some fields and disciplines have long histories of experiential learning. For over 100 years, for example, geographers have utilised field trips in order to use the land as their 'laboratory' and have a rich tradition of experiential learning in various forms. Similarly, education fields have long been associated with attempts to immerse students in school settings. This approach was built initially on the legacy of the settlement movement and pressure from Oxbridge students to experience 'social education' (Brewis, op cit) but has long been commonplace in the preparation of teaching professionals. This has included attempts to place students in schools in more challenging neighbourhoods in order to hone their classroom management skills, as well as attempts to create authentic classroom environments within higher education settings.

Placing trainee teachers in schools is an early example of work-based learning, which grew in prominence from the 1950s onwards and which was a distinctive element of much polytechnic education in the United Kingdom. Sandwich courses, where students would spend a year in industry in order to interweave theoretical and industrial knowledge, were the initial expression of this mode of higher education, but shorter-term placements and 'practicum' experiences also grew in popularity during the 1970s. This approach to the integration of theory and practice can also be associated with the literature on transferable skills, which grew during the same period. Although the idea of placing students in new and challenging settings is clearly a major theme throughout this handbook, the work-based learning movement was sponsored, both explicitly and implicitly, by the UK government at various stages in order to support the cause of economic growth. By ensuring that students gain understanding and skills that reflect the needs of dominant industrial interests, work-based learning helps prepare a workforce that's fit for purpose and that supports graduate employability. As we'll see in the case studies, these assumptions have been the foundations for a wide range of teaching and learning interventions. Where relationships between universities and industrial interests have really blossomed, a body of expertise has developed in relation to 'practice-informed learning', reflecting the advances in course content that have been achieved on the basis of effective partnership working (consider Guild HE, 2019). There are, however, other pedagogical traditions that can be associated with quite different principles and practices, leading to very different expressions of authenticity.

Pedagogical traditions associated with social justice would, we argue, take issue with the premises of the economic growth model. Rather than prioritise the needs of industry, or more broadly of Western capitalism, these traditions attempt to empower the learner as a citizen or change agent. They do not simply accept the dominant orthodoxy but rather seek to challenge it or to enable students to look at their personal situation through new lenses, potentially transforming their relationship with organisations, communities or society more generally. Service learning, for example, which developed initially in the United States in the early 1900s, integrates theoretical, classroom learning with experiential opportunities in community settings. In order to reflect on and develop understanding of conceptual knowledge, students 'give service' to community agencies or voluntary sector organisations. They then consider how their knowledge and understanding, of both themselves and their environment, shifted as a result of their placement. Service learning is now utilised in countries across the world, including the United Kingdom. Some versions of the approach continue to emphasise the virtues of active citizenship and the importance of giving and charitable endeavour, while others are more overtly political in the sense that they encourage the student to consider alternative pathways, for the individual students and for the communities with which they connect.

If service learning focuses on the individual and their potential contribution to communities, critical pedagogy considers political life at a deeper, more collective level. Inspired by the work of Paulo Freire (1970, 2013) and Henry Giroux (1988), critical pedagogy seeks to expose and unpack the power relationships inherent within contemporary society or even within education itself. Typically, critical pedagogy seeks to empower minority communities or those groups exploited or excluded in various ways by existing hierarchies. However, some critical pedagogies also position students as the minority interest and attempt to raise consciousness of the ways in which the university imposes meaning upon them. Students experiencing these modes of education might eventually demand greater say in the management of a university, an advance in democratic accountability by those in power positions, or greater responsibility for their own learning. By drawing parallels between the experiences of students and other minority or oppressed communities, the proponents of critical pedagogy help others unpack some of the aspects of contemporary society and its organisation that we might otherwise take for granted but which ultimately are there to promote and protect the interests of the powerful.

At first sight, the 'student-as-producer' approach shares a great deal with critical pedagogy. As Neary and Winn (2009) demonstrate, this approach seeks to resist the tendencies for students to conform to an idea of 'the consumer' engaged in a market relationship with a university and its staff, in which the value of the credentials concerned far outweighs the need for any genuinely educational interactions. Instead, student-as-producer attempts to refresh and invigorate these relationships by reviving the commitment to the unity of teaching and research. Students, in this view, shouldn't be mere recipients of research but should be empowered to become partners in the creation of knowledge. By engaging more directly, and by developing their knowledge through active research, students will gain a greater sense of ownership and identity and come to understand the basis of productive relationships. Their capability and confidence will also enable them to imagine alternative modes of organisation and to critique systems and practices which inhibit social justice and progressive politics.

In turn, student-as-producer is closely related to other attempts to move research and knowledge production to the centre of learning activity. Research engagement, inspired largely by the work of Healey and Jenkins (2009), has, since the 1990s, inspired academics across the world to find ways to integrate teaching with research and to engage students as active contributors to the process of knowledge production. This approach centres on interpretations of effective learning and how an empowered student is likely to be a more successful scholar with a wide range of transferable skills. It lacks the overt political intent that we might associate with student-as-producer modes but has nevertheless inspired many institutions to adapt their curricula to support opportunities for students to learn by doing research right from their very first arrival at university. A number of research-intensive institutions, most notably University College London, have made research engagement their 'signature' pedagogy, the focus of their strategic and professional development. The story of this process, together with a wide range of success stories from disciplines and departments, is told in Fung's (2017) work on the 'connected curriculum.'

Although they differ in relation to their value set and emphasis, all of these traditions or models promote authentic learning. They all create opportunities for students to learn in real world settings, to collaborate, to learn from staff and from their peers and to make an impact on their surroundings. They also, crucially, refuse to accept the curriculum in its current form and seek to innovate by reconsidering the various elements of experience that contribute to learning. In the next section, we contemplate the nature of the curriculum 'jigsaw' and consider the extent to which the pieces can be rearranged to create new and better versions of the university picture.

Components of the curriculum and the potential for re-design

Readers in most universities will be all too familiar with the call to prepare students more effectively for their entry to higher education. Transition periods such as inductions and welcome weeks are crucial periods, and it's widely acknowledged that learner identities and aspirations are at their most brittle at these moments (consider Tangey et al., 2018). We're therefore encouraged to 'tell the story' of universities so that students can understand the rules – both written and unwritten – of the institutions they enter. This is particularly important for those students from backgrounds where understanding and awareness of the purpose and culture of higher education is constrained.

However, in telling the story, the constructed and often arbitrary nature of much of institutional life frequently makes itself plain. We tend to organise our lives into semesters rather than terms, teach in small chunks or 'modules' or 'units', assess in certain ways and at certain times, have long summer holidays and defer to people with strange titles like 'dean' and 'vice chancellor.' If anyone takes the opportunity to ask why this is all in place, we may struggle to answer sensibly, and this is before we contemplate the ways in which fields of study are organised and located. While we all inhabit institutions that promise universality and collaboration, most of us remain in silos, reluctant to take the time to co-operate with others or too busy to look up from our daily concerns to see what else might be going on.

To a great extent, university timeframes reflect those of British education generally. The term structure in British schools owes its shape to the Victorian era and the need for families to have children available for agricultural work. Historically, university timetables have mirrored this approach. There have been a number of attempts to shift this basic three-term structure into more manageable 'semesters' since the 1980s. Organising the academic year in two equal halves makes some aspects of university business more manageable and is now the dominant mode at most institutions. However, some universities operate trimester approaches, imposing an additional period of learning in the summer months. Accepting all of the concerns about wellbeing and working conditions that emanate from these kinds of suggestions, we should recognise that these developments help us to ask meaningful questions about where and when learning takes place and how its advance can be best maximised and captured.

Within semesters or terms, learning tends to be organised into modules – discrete units of learning that are offered within a menu enabling students to make choices and build pathways. Modularisation has been a feature of UK higher education since the 1980s and has been presented as a mode which enables efficient delivery, facilitates mobility and credit exchange and enhances choice. It's to be distinguished from the previous approach where courses were essentially linear, with topics following each other and knowledge building incrementally. Modular learning implies greater flexibility, with units of learning combining in order to suit the needs of the student rather than the academic expert. As self-standing, credit-bearing units of learning, modules also tend to contain assessments, so study and achievement become tightly entwined. Although some institutions have attempted to disentangle learning from assessment, most universities remain dominated by this couplet. Critics of modular approaches therefore highlight the dangers of instrumentalism, with students learning 'to-the-test' rather than being motivated by more intrinsic concerns. They also point to the fragmented nature of course design, with some degrees made up from largely disconnected elements that tend to reflect narrow academic interests rather than a coherent overall package (French, 2015).

Modular degrees can indeed be something of a straightjacket, but there are ways to work with the structures that may enable us to find a way around their constraints. Many universities are currently engaged in curriculum transformations or re-writes, which reflect a desire for design processes to emphasise graduate outcomes and attributes. While these processes can help us to ask fundamental questions about the purpose of degree programmes, they also give voice to those who are prepared to ask about the size, timing and location of modules. We may not all be able to wriggle free from modularisation, but we can ask whether 'block' provision – over a full week, for example – might be more effective than short episodes of two hours or so, scheduled once a week over a four-month period. Learning could, in fact, be organised across all kinds of schedules to suit learners and to support their development. Similarly, certain credit sizes for modules may suit organisational requirements and procedures, but other sizes may be more advantageous for student learning and may help to reduce the emphasis on high-stakes final assessments or to enable more effective synthesis between different elements. Reorganising and restructuring modules may also help to connect formal learning to other aspects of the student experience, such as induction or transition periods or to work and volunteering contexts.

A central premise of this text is the idea that effective learning can and does take place beyond the campus boundaries. This can relate to the individuals who are allocated work or community placements or research tasks or projects. It can also relate to entire modules being delivered in new settings, in the local community or economy or in 'field' or 'industry' locations. The nature of the student experience in these modules will depend on the intended learning outcomes of the module, which may prioritise disciplinary knowledge but may also emphasise particular skills – witness, for example, the tendency to create separate provision for research methods in the majority of degree programmes. Depending on the overall aims of a programme or course, it may be perfectly legitimate to incorporate modules that are organised around the acquisition of particular skills or capabilities, which focus on the application of knowledge rather than simply its acquisition or which prioritise the building of cohort identity or confidence. There's a tendency within modularised learning to cram everything into each contributing unit – content knowledge, transferable skills, application, employability, citizenship – but it's not always necessary or desirable. Smart course design can clarify purpose, save time, use space effectively and enhance learning, but it may lead to provision taking on a different character to that to which we're accustomed.

For many academics, the idea that the students themselves might take on aspects of course delivery is disconcerting. Most lecturers studied at a time when notions of competence were irrevocably entwined with subject expertise – a rigorous, intellectually challenging educational experience was led by those with deepest, most contemporary knowledge. However, by breaking up the educational journey into its component elements, we begin to see that there are roles for all kinds of stakeholders in the process. Indeed, authentic learning tends towards a redefinition of how we define expertise and who has power and the ability to exert influence in this context. While earlier in this chapter, we noted the desire of different pedagogical traditions to empower the learner and to find ways to engage students as co-producers of knowledge, we also wish to acknowledge the work of institutions to develop support schemes to help students play a more prominent role in the curriculum. The students-as-partners movement, best summarised by Healey et al. (2014), reflects the work of a range of institutions to support students in representative capacities but also as teachers, coaches, facilitators and mentors. Peer-assisted learning initiatives are prominent at universities of all kinds across the sector, in some cases offering support beyond the formal curriculum but in others enabling students to play an active role within modules and also receiving academic credit that recognises the development of their own capacities as part of the process.

If it's possible, and in many cases desirable, to reorganise some of the components of higher education, then we have to address the next concerns of the academic community, which will relate to how and when these experiences are assessed and accredited.

Knowledge, skills, action and assessment

Students experience assessment for a variety of reasons. In some contexts, assessment is a measure of progress, identifying the position of the learner and what can be done to enhance their understanding and experience. In others, assessment will be designed to provide a focus for the particular learning experience and act as a motivational force, which could be competitive or co-operative in emphasis. There are then settings where assessment will essentially be designed to rank students so that supply lines to vocations or professions can be managed. Forms of ranking are a consequence of a society that espouses merit as the key criterion for respect or acknowledgement, but they're often criticised on the basis of their tendency to encourage instrumental approaches to study and superficial or 'surface' learning.

Our emphasis in this section will be on 'assessment for learning', those forms of interaction and evaluation that are designed in order to encourage more meaningful engagement in a curriculum, which enable students to enter into conversations with their assessors rather than have assessment imposed upon them and which enable a wider community of actors to support the students as they progress. This approach is often closely associated with formative assessment, where students receive largely informal feedback from staff, their peers or forms of self-testing. Assessment for learning is constructivist in nature; it enables the learner to reflect on their learning and to begin to understand the particular conditions in which they learn most effectively. Because the approach dilutes the authority of the academic by enabling other stakeholders to participate in the process, it's suited to those pedagogical traditions that seek to involve those beyond the established disciplinary communities.

Since the 1990s, the relationship between learning outcomes and assessment tasks has been seen as central to effective curriculum design (Biggs and Tang, 2011). Constructive alignment describes the extent to which all of the learning experiences of the student lead to the achievement of the learning outcomes determined at the outset. This is in contrast to traditional approaches, where a mismatch between the learning outcomes and intended assessment task was often evident. The overuse of formal examinations to test understanding, rather than the recollection to which they are more suited, is an oft-cited example of this conflict.

Many of the capabilities that we consider in this handbook are new to higher education, reflecting alternative bodies of knowledge that have gained prevalence in other sectors. However, the learning for assessment framework offers us most of the tools that we need in order to understand how best to inform, enhance and evaluate the progress of students. As we have seen, authentic learning in higher education will be designed with one or more of the following outcomes in mind:

1   The application of knowledge to a real-life setting or context. While this has the potential of engaging the learner more effectively with their learning, it also carries the possibility of greater stretch, challenge and validity – in the sense that the ability to apply can be easier to identify and discern than the ability to understand (see Race, 2006; Knight and Yorke, 2003).
2   The production of knowledge for use by internal and/or external stakeholders.
3   The development of specified capacities or skills that can't be achieved through traditional modes of learning.
4   Enabling the student to learn about the language, expectations or culture of an organisational context beyond the university, with a view to future engagement with a profession, sector or community.
5   Enhancing the self-efficacy of the student, supporting the development of their identity as a student and member of a learning or subject community (see Baxter Magolda, 1999, 1992; Baxter Magolda and Hall, 2017).
6   Empowering the student by extending their sense of agency and purpose, extending their network and building their social and cultural capital. In turn, this creates space for them to experiment, to take risks and to be creative.

In most cases, there are relatively straightforward connections to be made between intended outcomes and forms of assessment. The exception is that most forms of assessment don't adequately cope with the potential failure of a student, in the sense that established assessments are part of our meritocratic structures. They mitigate against risk taking and against the production of new or alternative approaches. However much a lecturer may say that they seek to encourage innovation and a 'strike against the status quo', they will struggle to support this if their learning outcomes are written in a restrictive way. This is of some importance if we take seriously those who argue that failure is an important part of learning, particularly for those who wish to innovate or to lead. Our challenge is therefore how to overcome this conundrum; we need to encourage students to be bold and risk failure in their experiments and adventures, but we can't run the risk of them failing their assessments as a result. We also need to acknowledge the possibility that in enhancing student agency, we open up the possibility of other unintended outcomes. By asserting tight control over the curriculum and over the experiences of students, we stand a good chance of predicting and managing their outcomes. As soon as we begin to release control and invite other variables into the equation, we open up the possibility of eventualities that we can't predict. If we wish to promote innovation and enterprise, we'll need assessment regimes that take account of these potential anomalies.

One response to these challenges of assessment is to make clear the distinction between process and product. In some cases, course design will emphasise the benefits that are to be derived from student participation in a process. This will often be the case with experiential approaches, which carry with them the expectation that students will learn from the challenges they face on their particular journey and from others with whom they engage and that they'll also learn from their own responses to incidents and accidents. In these instances, reflective practice is a body of knowledge that can be deployed in order to assess the effectiveness of the experience. Moon's (2004, 1999) work provides a useful summary of this approach, which is now established across disciplinary boundaries and at all kinds of institution. It provides a body of knowledge through which to assess the interrelationship between action and learning, and carries the potential to enable students to take risks, to challenge the status quo and, in principle, to fail. Reflective assessments focus on what might be learnt from the cycle of experiment and failure; they don't impose penalties on those who stretch the boundaries only to fall at the final hurdle. They suit open processes where we relinquish control of the learning environment, where we no longer have the need to restrict the outcomes of an experience for the student.

Reflective practice tends towards assessments that summarise, analyse and synthesise the outcomes of experiences and that consider the relationships between theoretical constructs and the applied context. Typically, a reflective account would be a written essay, report or narrative, but it can take a verbal or oral form and can be mediated by technology in various ways. Substantiation of experiences is often provided through a reflective diary from which data is drawn or through 'artefacts' collected on the course of the journey. Reflections and artefacts can be stored in a portfolio, increasingly electronic, and then drawn upon to construct an overarching narrative.

This approach differs considerably from those where the outcomes of a learning episode relate directly to the creation of a product of some kind or the demonstration of a skill or a body of knowledge that has been acquired. In many of the traditions that we've explored, an explicit or implicit assumption is that students play a part in the continued construction and development of knowledge. In order to do this, there's an expectation that they produce outputs of value to their academic community or to other internal or external stakeholders. These outputs may relate to the process of research, so they may be elements of academic papers – abstracts, literature reviews, data analyses, annotated bibliographies, for example – or they may reflect other forms of academic communication, such as presentations, posters or the viva-voce. They may alternatively relate to modes of communication more prominent in other organisations, for example, audits or evaluations, or reports to commissioners, boards or committees. The advance of technologies is continually opening up new forms of communication that can be utilised in these settings, from narrated PowerPoint presentations to podcasts and vodcasts, to exhibitions (both real and virtual) and events, festivals and celebrations.

While these forms of production require appropriate capabilities, another approach would be to identify the particular element of knowledge or skill that's demanded and to enable the student to perform it in an appropriate and meaningful context. This would mean directly assessing the capability in question and having both criteria and personnel in place at the right time to judge the success or otherwise of the student. The direct assessment of performance does, of course, have a long history in subjects like drama, music and physical education. All of the approaches we've considered carry with them the potential for those beyond established academic communities to contribute to assessment in some way. Peers, colleagues, external stakeholders and communities can, in various ways, contribute to the design of learning experiences and their intended outputs, to their delivery and to their eventual assessment.

Conclusion

In this chapter, we've attempted to unpack some of the key aspects of the learning experiences of higher education. We've done this to encourage you to recognise the arbitrary and constructed nature of much of our work in universities. In order to make sense of our busy lives, we accept the majority of these ideas and structures without question, but it serves us well to consider, from time to time, whether they're actually sensible and whether there might be other ways to approach some of the challenges that we face.

To help us to look afresh at the various pieces of the university jigsaw, we've contrasted the classical, traditional approach to learning with the key principles of other, more radical traditions. We've explored the new forms of learning that are gradually becoming respected and accepted within universities and considered how and why these forms of knowledge might be usefully assessed. We have, additionally, extended our analysis to consider the ways in which learning in higher education might become more open and collaborative and embrace new partners in the processes of design, construction and delivery. Authentic learning carries democratising potential and the possibility of a greater say for students, for other staff in universities and for external stakeholders and communities.

Chapter 3

Working in partnership

Introduction

This chapter explores what authentic learning entails for university partners. It builds on earlier chapters and the observations we have already made around who and what universities are for, knowledge as power and the function of education in both reinforcing inequality or disrupting and challenging it. However in this chapter, we aim to go a little bit further and look more deeply into relationships and partnerships and the ethical dimension of these. We will look at the different purposes that partnerships can serve and provide a set of ideas to help you reflect on what makes for effective partnerships. We will also be looking at 'the baggage' that universities, their staff and students can bring into their relationships.

In so many of the interviews we conducted for this book, it was evident that the time it took to develop relationships with external and internal partners was by far the most resource-intensive aspect of the work. It was also often cited as the most rewarding aspect. We'll therefore explore the benefits and challenges that you might expect from partnership work and how you might justify to others the investment of time and resource needed for building mutually beneficial partnerships.

This chapter aims to provide insight into some of the very practical questions you might face, questions such as:

- How do you effectively identify which organisations to partner with and why?
- How do you create alignment with partners around your teaching and/ or research priorities?
- How do you build relationship capital and work in ways that foster mutual benefit for students, the university, partners and their respective communities?
- What structures are needed to maintain effective partnerships?

Authentic learning is only possible with a context. This chapter is about that context and the position of learners within it. In short, we want to look under the bonnet of partnership work. The chapter is relevant to working with both internal partners, for example, a library or department within the university, and external partners, for example, businesses, community groups, charities and so on, although largely we focus on the latter. As with other chapters, we will draw on the literature and ideas we've found most useful and give some air time to some of the issues that tend to surface in partnership and some that don't surface but lurk underneath. The chapter is organised around a number of short sections:

- The importance of partnership work
- Who you partner with and why your motivations matter
- The different capacities to partner
- Seeking and generating alignment in partnership work
- Can you be too close to a partner?
- Navigating ethics and boundary critique

Our overall aim is to provide food for thought and to highlight in a useful way some of the grit and heavy lifting involved in making authentic learning work.

The importance of partnership work

Human relationships matter. This is true to every one of our creative endeavours, including education and research. In science, we've recently moved away from a conceptualisation of the lone scientist 'hero', working in the lab (Clark, 2017) – the researcher as an objective, unfeeling individual, who is removed from society and the implications of his work. Whilst there is little doubt that in the pursuit of new knowledge, we need to get our heads down; that the scientific method requires discipline and objectivity and that sometimes isolation is required, there is also little doubt that society needs research to have integrity, that it needs be connected and involved. These days, collaboration appears to be in vogue. Whilst great minds of the past such as Newton were purported to have spent a great deal of time working alone, looking down on their contemporaries and worrying about the theft of their ideas, it's now often argued that the best science is often done in multinational, multidisciplinary teams (Adams, 2013; Clark, 2017).

Similar leanings are emerging when we look at the adoption and distribution of new ideas in society. Here we have moved from a 'push' model, where innovation is dispersed from highly specialised research units into society, towards a model where the interplay between these units and society is thought about in ever more sophisticated ways. Other players (such as business, local and central government, the voluntary and community sectors etc.) do not only have a role in generating new knowledge and can help shape the direction of research. There is also a need to develop the capacity of regions, places, communities and businesses to apply knowledge and innovation in their respective worlds (Brennan et al., 2013; Jongbloed et al., 2008).

In education, too, if the early 2000s were dominated by a focus on employability and skills, the next decade will see us moving further away from the academic 'sage on the stage' model to a more holistic approach where a greater range of players and experiences constitute a societally orientated undergraduate and postgraduate education. It is here where authentic learning comes in. As authentic learning is situated in real life, the challenges and contexts that students are faced with will offer a far broader set of complexities, uncertainties and interdependencies than many theory-based or 'simulated' projects.

Consider two students working on the same research question; however, one student is working on a brief that was developed by an academic tutor and is largely imagined, and the other is working on a brief designed by a client or partners. The latter student will be exposed to circumstances where they encounter multiple stakeholders and multiple perspectives, and any effort to apply theoretical knowledge within such circumstances will be met with both the push and pull that is present in all human interaction. It is here that theory meets practice. In so doing, praxis knowledge – that is, "theoretically engaged action" (Horner, 2016: 18) – can arise. Such knowledge is rooted in a reciprocal process of reflection/action/action/reflection (Burke et al., 2017), with theory and practice informing and strengthening one another. Theory may support practitioners to see and understand things in new ways, whilst practice can challenge theoretical assumptions, provoking deeper, more rigorous thought. It is the mutuality that is core, for, as Freire (1970) counsels, reflection without action is verbalism and action without reflection activism.

There have been a number of recent policy shifts that have brought to the forefront the need for partnership work in how we learn and innovate. For example, in research funding, we've seen a recent drive to address societal challenges (i.e. health, food security, climate change etc.), offering a radically different framing for the way we think about research and its application. They require universities to form teams of experts with different knowledge bases, including experts in experience (e.g. users, consumers, policy makers etc.). All sides involved are challenged to question the context of the problem and push themselves and others to think differently about solutions, asking different questions that open up thinking and possibility rather than working in silos or trying to provide 'quick fixes' (Smolovic-Jones and Jacklin-Jarvis, 2016a). Key recent UK policy drivers around this include:

- The UK Research and Innovation (UKRI) Industrial Strategy Challenge Fund, which directs funding at societal challenges (UKRI, 2020a)
- The evolving Knowledge Exchange Framework, a commission from the government which is led by Research England (which includes 'local

growth and regeneration' and 'public and community engagement' as key perspectives) (UKRI, 2020b)

- UKRI's Strength in Places Fund, a place-based approach to research and innovation funding to support significant local economic growth
- Higher Education Funding Council Wales (HEFCW) Civic Mission activity (HEFCW, 2018)
- UKRI's public engagement strategy (UKRI, 2020d)

Societal challenges also offer up a different frame for education, teaching and learning. Sometimes, however, the problems that society poses may appear to be less 'academically rich', and it is this that acts as a barrier to many academics taking up authentic learning in their teaching practices. Yet whilst their richness may not immediately lie in theory or foundational knowledge, it abounds in the context in which the problems originate. For example, take this observation from Anderson and Priest (2017) in writing about 'live projects' (see Case Study 14 for more information):

> Students who had undertaken live projects reported a strong sense of community and a recurring comment was typically expressed thus: 'it helped designing for a community that you could interact with'. One student achieved a level of insight not normally possible at this stage because they noticed that they had fallen into a common trap for designers of becoming so absorbed in the fascination of making that the needs of the client and site had been neglected.
>
> (Anderson and Priest, 2017: 187)

Our current trajectory will take us further from didactic academic/tutor-led education. It will also move us beyond student-centred education which, although it brought many valuable innovations such as peer-to-peer learning and students as producers, is still missing the value of networks and partnerships to student learning in higher education and higher education's role within society.

Who you partner with and why your motivations matter

When it comes to partnering, we can create a divide between universities and partners through the concept of positionality. This concept describes identity "in terms of an insider-outsider perspective, based on the researchers' relationship to the specific research setting and community" (Muhammad et al., 2015: 1048). Figure 3.1 neatly presents four ways of positioning partners in terms of doing "to", "for", "with", or "alongside". It should be noted that these positions are not necessarily arrived at through conscious deliberative choice and ofttimes can be arrived at by simply not questioning the perspectives or motives that one brings to a partnership. Academics

Action	Perspective
Doing TO the 'other'	Pity – providing something whether or not there is a want or need for it
Doing FOR the 'other'	Sympathy – a want or need is expressed that you fulfil
Doing WITH the 'other'	Empathy – building capacity on both sides of the partnership to achieve a given end
Doing ALONGSIDE the 'other'	Solidarity – where you act towards a shared, common goal as one; differences between partners dissolve

Figure 3.1 Ways of positioning partners (Fletcher, 2019)

may often be perceived to enter communities as relative outsiders due to the privileged and powerful status of universities within wider society (Kerstetter, 2012). Conversely, communities are usually relative insiders due to their insight into the unique issues that they face.

Such framing can be unhelpful, particularly when it masks the multiple identities of the people involved in partnership work. For example, in practice, the lead contact for a partnering organisation may be university educated, a university alumnus/alumna and adult learner or researcher and may also therefore be outside the communities they are representing, albeit closer than the students or academics. Though a student may be part of the community in which the programme is based, an academic might live in the neighbourhood in question and be deeply motivated by the issue the programme seeks to address. So, positionalities are complicated; the interrelations around partnership work are often messier than we can portray in this discussion. However, a cognisance of your relative 'insider' or 'outsider' status and how this impacts your experience of the partnership may be helpful.

An outsider/insider dynamic can create a false dichotomy around the beneficiaries of authentic learning, describing it as a 'win-win' for partners and students without testing these assumptions. Research has shown that this framing significantly diminishes the role of the partner and the assets they bring to the partnership (Stoecker et al., 2009). It portrays them as beneficiaries without really unpacking their contribution to this work. In a way, this speaks to how we view or position the 'other' in a partnership, for our perspectives of them drive our actions, as follows:

Many working in and with civil society[1] organisations believe it to be part of their mission to help students understand the issues facing their clients. Others engage with authentic learning because they want access to other resources that the university has to offer (e.g. research departments, buildings and infrastructure), and student placements are taken on as part of a wider exchange (Stoecker et al., 2009). Understanding at the outset the motivations of partners will invariably inform how you manage expectations and can help reduce complications further down the line.

The different capacities to partner

There is a risk when developing real world programmes that we focus too greatly on the role of theory and the role of context as too-isolated entities. In this model, the purpose of the context is only to serve the development of new knowledge for the student. For example, students might apply their research methods in a consultancy project and then might get assessed on their application of those research methods. By focusing only on course-based theory and technical knowledge of how to apply that theory, students will miss deepening their understanding of the social contexts in which they find themselves. In this model, placements are nothing more than a 'living lab' to test new ideas; a university is operating in extraction mode, taking as much value from society without putting back in.

The capacity to partner – the availability of resources such as time and money – will vary across organisations. Previous research has stressed the need for universities to:

- Develop the infrastructure needed to create high-quality collaborative research partnerships
- Recognise that it takes time to build trust
- Take explicit steps to mitigate the risk of enhancing inequalities through collaboration
- Focus on developing sustainable institutions and practices that are able to meet the desire for public learning across all parties involved
  (NCCPE, 2019; Facer and Enright, 2016)

Universities often partner with organisations that are different from themselves in how they are governed, how they are organised, how decisions are made and in terms of funding and resources. A community group working with homeless people seeking shelter will typically be working in a hand-to-mouth way, faced with immediate, sometimes life-depending decisions. They are established as responsive to the needs of their service users and expend great energy in ensuring that someone has a bed for the night. Whilst they can see the benefits of more long-term, strategic work, the pressures of the here and now may delimit their desire to develop a collaborative student project.

Differences may relate to power and equality. These can arise in a number of ways but most notably with relation to funding and capacity. Authentic learning approaches are presented as invites from universities to external organisations to engage. As such, universities have the power to structure the invite, to condition it within the bounds of their existing order (Leal, 2007). In other words, they set the terms of engagement and in ways that reinforce power differentials. For example, many partners who host student projects do not get paid to do so, whereas universities often employ paid academics to teach the students and sometimes even have placement managers to broker relationships.

Partners on authentic learning projects may invest time in supervising, training and managing the quality of outputs, with this time usually given in kind. Very few organisations can absorb such 'load' without impacting their core services. Ethical issues arise here. Is it really fair to entangle organisations in authentic learning opportunities which may detract from their day-to-day operations upon which the wellbeing of service users may be contingent? Certainly, a note of caution should be sounded and external partners fully supported to make a conscious decision as to the benefits and otherwise of potential engagement.

The National Coordinating Centre for Public Engagement's (NCCPE) Community Partner Network has identified a number of key issues to watch out for in partnering. Whilst developed by and for partners working in smaller organisations and community groups, the list acts a useful reminder that despite good intentions, partnership working can be frustrating, particularly for those working with the university but also for those working within the university trying to circumvent such issues:

- Bureaucracy – universities are large institutions and can be unwieldy to work with easily
- Incomplete information about what universities could potentially offer means community partners cannot 'trade' in order to get the best out of the partnership and vice versa
- Universities can sometimes think they do not need to offer anything in return or offer too little
- Universities do not always try hard enough to support community ideas, overcome obstacles or adapt agendas to better meet community interests
- Expect complications over finances – little or no money may be available for the community partner, and even if it is, university payment systems can prove complex and slow
- Expertise can be valued differently, with textbook knowledge often reified over grassroots experience
- Academics can be threatened by non-academics knowing more than they do

NCCPE and UK Community Partner Network (2020)

Whether we're working with a business or civil society group, partnerships are often navigated at an individual level. This means that should any one individual move on or change roles, a project can come to an abrupt halt. Subsequently, universities are increasingly trying to develop more long-term, strategic partnerships. Such partnerships are often built around what was once an ad-hoc project that responded to the conditions on the ground but has been sustained and developed over time. For example, the University of Cardiff's Community Gateway programme now has more than 48 community-university projects in and around Grangetown (University of Cardiff, 2020). Authentic learning projects may start as ad hoc or one off (even if repeated for several years) around shared goals negotiated at an individual level but may evolve into a wider programme or strategic approach with activity occurring across multiple departments, underpinned by high levels of trust, resource and capability sharing, alongside formal and standardised collaboration and co-operative arrangements.

On the one hand, strategic partnerships at an institutional level are required to address complex, long-term issues. On the other, most authentic learning projects are short-term, discrete activities, dependent on and susceptible to the goodwill and connections of the people involved. However, as Smolovic-Jones and Jacklin-Jarvis (2016b) contend, it is possible to think about such a dilemma in a different way, conceiving partnerships as part of a 'collaborative fabric.' Here, multiple projects and practices make up the collaborative whole – those authentic learning projects that are unexpected, creative, serendipitous alongside those that are purposeful, planned and intentional. So the collaborative fabric is always evolving, always unfinished, subject to internal and external pressures, yet it is possible to position every authentic learning project as woven into a wider whole.

On both sides of partnership, relationship brokers play a valuable role in traversing the norms, cultures and values of different spheres and helping to link their own internal networks with external networks and resources such as the university. They often provide a 'gearing system' between two or more organisations, bringing with them a deep and rich understanding of the way things work within their community, the language used, the typical behaviours and responses. And with that comes knowledge of how to navigate these in order to create a partnership around shared goals. They unlock the actual and potential resources embedded within a partnership, including aspects such as knowledge (what people know), attitudes (what people think), networks (who people know) and skills and resources (what people have and can do). Putman (2000) describes these combined assets as social capital.

Seeking and generating alignment in partnership work

Our natural propensity to work with those like us (McPherson et al., 2001; Harari, 2014) dictates that many partnerships in authentic learning programmes are built around people where there is already a degree of shared understanding and social capital. Pragmatically, a certain degree of similarity is needed for partnerships to gel, build trust and work with each other effectively. Pierre Bourdieu's work highlights some of the ethical risks here and how social capital is used to produce and reproduce inequality by reinforcing circles of power and influence via 1) socialised dispositions which shape whether someone experiences a group as being 'for me'; 2) the cultural, social and economic hand that you can play in the group (i.e. your actual resources) and 3) the different institutional arrangements which shape the rules of the relationship and positionings in the group.

Where the purpose of authentic learning is to bring together different forms of knowledge and to work across different boundaries, whether these be disciplinary, institutional or cultural, combining different forms isn't a straightforward task, as partners bring their own sets of institutional practices, preconceived ideas, expectations and personal histories. Yet such differences can generate moments of tension that serve a pedagogical function, with divergent knowledges and experiences providing opportunities for deliberation and learning (Nichols et al., 2013). Difference can act as a portal, a threshold, to new perspectives, and on encountering it, individuals may, according to Land et al. (2014), pass through the following progressive stages:

1   The learner encounters and integrates something new;
2   Subsequently, the learner recognises shortcomings in their existing view of the phenomenon in question;
3   The learner lets go of their older view;
4   The learner lets go of their earlier mode of subjectivity;
5   The learner envisages, and ultimately accepts, an alternative version of self.

Authentic learning projects usually start in one of three key ways:

• A partner approaches a university with a request or question;
• A department approaches a partner with an offer or idea;
• A department and/or partner work together from the outset to develop a proposal.

Whichever the origination, tutors look for projects that are academically robust and sufficiently testing of students' skills, knowledge and experiences; they also seek reassurance that a partner can offer a good experience to the student and can meet certain requirements for support. Partners still look for projects and students that add value to their direct organisational needs. These might not be core business needs (for example, a student would not typically be involved in drawing up a local charity's fundraising strategy, but they might conduct research that informs it development), but they will necessarily be issues that the organisation wants to explore. Students are often looking for opportunities that are meaningful to them and their personal and professional interests.

One challenge to navigate is how to align the problem that an external partner is seeking to address with an academic project. For some projects, this is about making the question larger via the application of theories or concepts that allow for critical reflection and the generation of praxis knowledge. Here, the goal is to avoid focus purely on instrumental, task-oriented activities devoid of critical reflection. For example, a client might be interested in how many visitors a local park receives, how long they stay and how they use the space. This alone is an instrumental, observation task and would be too straightforward for a third-year undergraduate dissertation in social policy; there might be potential for a first-year module provided some room for critical refection on the observations. To make it more appropriate for a student dissertation, the project would need a stronger theoretical grounding and perhaps a bigger dataset. The student could conduct some benchmarking research into use of public spaces in a number of neighbouring sites, perhaps using secondary data from the council. For other projects, you may need to make the scope much smaller in order for it to be deliverable within the curriculum.

Challenges of alignment can play out within the project or piece of work that a student is delivering as described previously but are often magnified within assessment even if sufficiently addressed during the problem definition phase. For students, assessment criteria can provide guidance for their learning and allow them to monitor their progress, but ultimately, they indicate the standards which will be used to judge performance. However, there can sometimes be insufficient consideration of assessment standards for authentic learning and how these need to be adjusted to take into account partnership work. This is particularly the case where authentic learning is 'bolted-on' to existing modules (Owen and Hill, 2011).

In setting up an authentic learning project, it is therefore crucial to begin with an understanding of what is already known about a given issue. Sometimes students complete this as part of an initial scoping exercise. The template subsequently is a simple one but can really help, once the problem has been defined, to surface what partners already know about the subject. It can also help navigate tensions over an academic project (primarily concerned with foundational knowledge) and a client project (primarily concerned with praxis knowledge applicable to business needs).

- Description of the problem
- What do we know already about the external partner?
- What do want to find out?
- What data do we have already?
- What are the underpinning theoretical ideas that might inform this work?

Can you be too close to a partner?

Boschma (2005) provides a useful framing for evaluating and reflecting on whether a potential project partner is right for your programme. His framework describes five domains through which you can access a potential partnership as being too close, too far or about right. These dimensions of proximity are cognitive, geographical, organisational, social and institutional.

Geographical proximity relates to the distance between partners. Quite often, authentic learning occurs with partners that are geographically close to the university, but opportunities can arise that are further afield. Geographical distance may create challenges for students in terms of travel to and from a partner and the cost of such travel. This may put a project at risk further down the line and make it more vulnerable to failure as other competing demands arise for a student's time. It also brings with it cost and budget implications for both the partner and the student. Equally, if working in close geographical proximity, there may be times when a project is too close. This is the case with many internal authentic learning projects (e.g. where a student conducts a placement in a university faculty, for example) and may contribute to an insufficiently challenging placement in terms of working across cultures and difference (were this to be an aim of the programme).

Organisational proximity refers to the arrangements that are in place between organisations to enable learning across and within. It refers to the capacity to participate in and nurture networks that feed and develop a project or initiative. Organisations with close organisational proximity to universities, like other universities or large publicly funded institutions, may have greater capacity to participate in networks and project meetings that relate to an initiative than small community groups or commercial entities.

Social proximity refers to the trust and ties between individual actors within a partnership. This occurs at an individual level. You may find, for example, if you're an academic with direct lived or professional experience of the domain (e.g. mental health, drug use, environmental concerns, young people etc.), you've greater social proximity to the key partners working in this space than an academic who has no prior experience. This relates to you being able to read and interpret the norms, values and cultural practices of the partner.

Institutional proximity refers to the norms and values of the institutions and their respective differences. For example, universities and other large publicly funded organisations will be more closely related in their institutional arrangements than, say, a university and local advocacy group or a multinational.

Cognitive proximity refers to the degree to which partners are close within their knowledge bases. As a rule, organisations are more likely to identify, interpret and exploit knowledge that is familiar but distinct from what they already know. A project that's located across a large gap in cognitive proximity will require process and investment to bridge the gap. This might require, for example, several meetings upfront, workshops with key stakeholders to help understand issues or even preliminary research. On the contrary, where the cognitive gap is too small, an authentic learning programme may be much easier to manage, but its impact may be negligible. This can often result in students feeling disempowered or undermotivated, as their work will make very little contribution to the field.

You can use this framework to reflect on with whom you might partner, challenges that may result as a result of your relative proximity and steps that you might take to adjust proximity towards optimal levels. For example, if the cognitive proximity is too distant at the outset, you might look to develop a number of exchange meetings or workshops with the partner to gain a better understanding of their current knowledge of a given issue and to map this across your research and teaching interests. Where geographical proximity is too far, you might introduce online meetings and telephone conferences to conduct meetings and negate distance.

Navigating ethics and boundary critique

When working in partnership, there are number of ethical issues to consider as part of your work around the choice of partner, their field of work, the nature of your project and the quality of interaction. Each university will have its own procedures and regulations for ethical approval around authentic learning, and if the project relates to work with vulnerable adults or young people, this will raise specific issues for ethical consent.

Whilst ethical procedures will already be in place for your research, if you're just getting started in authentic learning and do not have established relationships or procedures for educational work, this will require attention. We've found in our case study work that in some instances, the need for ethical approval and concerns of the resource and time needed to gain approval have led some authentic learning projects to change their focus and work with fewer partners or deliver projects where there's less risk. Other issues that might arise revolve around the choice of partner – for example, how their business practices might align with or contravene university policy, as in the case of disinvestment policies. Equally, if the groups you're working with harbour radical or hardline views, you may need to consider policies on platforming and the educational framework that surround the project.

Whatever the specific arrangements needed for ethical approval, we recommend that you develop an ethical framework that sits across your authentic learning programme. You can view examples of ethical frameworks online – for example, the Kings Fund's collaboration policy. Such frameworks usually set out the rationale for partnerships, some guiding principles (for example, the Kings Fund's are independence, mutual respect, integrity and transparency, shared goals for better health, procedures for navigating conflicts of interest) and the expectations for partners (Kings Fund, 2020). Ethical frameworks should focus on institutional arrangements and the quality of relationships themselves. The Centre for Social Justice and Community Action at Durham University has one such framework that incorporates both aspects well. It has produced a set of ethical principles which it describes as general standards or norms to promote as worthy or valuable for the flourishing of humans and/or the whole ecosystem (Durham University and NCCPE, 2012).

Whether you're working with a community group, local government or regional office of a multinational industry, it is clear that there will be differentials of power and agency between partners and the university. Power can, of course, have many different meanings and definitions, but broadly speaking, Huxham and Vangen (2005) speak of power in one of three ways:

- Power over – control over other people through, for example, direct political control or control over resources. Here, the emphasis is on your own gain. 'Power over' does not necessarily have to be overt, as when people internalise as 'natural' their power relations with others.
- Power to – having the capacities and capabilities to make choices and engage in actions; in other words, the ability to change the conditions of one's existence. Here, power is used for mutual gain, with individual power extended through interorganisational connections. Power to often embodies resistance to power over.
- Power for – altruistic gain in which, through partnership, power is 'transferred' to the 'other', building their capacity for action.

These frames for power operate at the macro level; that is, they are concerned with how organisations wield power over others based on structural position, resources, discourses and more. Yet this negates the import of 'micro-power' (Huxham and Beech, 2008), power at the relational level where individuals make a difference through discourse and meaning making. Huxham and Beech argue that micro-power is integral to processes of joint working and plays out in the minutiae of the day-to-day, from who arranges the time, location and format of partnership meetings through to who has 'final say' when challenges arise.

Everyday interactions and conversations therefore provide sites where people can seize micro-power and demonstrate leadership, enacting their agency. Agency is defined as 'the degree to which agents are free to make their own decisions and follow their chosen path of action.' Von Foerster proposed a view on ethics which was based on the importance of enabling human beings to become the best they can be, unrestrained by the negative impact of the choices of others. He summarised his view that to act ethically is to "act always to increase the number of choices" that someone has (von Foerster, 2003: 295).

As we noted earlier in this chapter, external partners are involved in authentic learning projects at the invite of universities, and, as such, universities set the terms of engagement. The agency of external partners may only be illusory. For example, within service-learning programmes, Butin (2010) notes the phenomenon of 'boutique multiculturalism', that is, the resistance of faculty to cultural values (knowledge, skills and dispositions) counter to their own or those they are attempting to foster in their students. Essentially, faculty may tolerate community perspectives up to a point, that point being where the 'other' offends their own internal and hidden norms.

Wherever there is inclusion in a partnership, there will also be exclusion. If you're working with a gatekeeper, they will not be representative of the community but will, if you're lucky, be able to help you navigate a way to that community. Many gatekeepers we've worked with find it deeply uncomfortable when they are treated as though they are representative of a wider community. But there will also be those that look to maintain local power differentials, using practices of participation to further their own influence and to reinforce their power, a charge often levelled at charity workers (Horner, 2016).

In any authentic learning partnership, you'll need to make boundary judgements about the 'facts' and 'norms' that are considered relevant and those considered less important, decisions imbued with power. Such judgements are informed by the reference systems we develop, the people we make these judgements alongside. It's important to critique these judgements and question the values and motives that inform our view of a situation and what it means to 'improve' it.

Conclusion

In this chapter, we've reviewed several dimensions of partnership work and how this impacts authentic learning. We've looked into the strategic value of partnerships and how these are becoming increasingly important within higher education policy to enhance research and teaching. We've unpacked the resource differences and power differentials that exist in partnership work. And we've looked at how you seek to generate alignment in partnership, including the pitfalls of being too close or too distant.

Too often, universities can default to working in 'extraction mode', taking from communities to further their own interests. This mode serves only short-term gains, depleting trust and the warmth that communities feel towards their local university. Taking the long view is harder work. Those that do this will often have to battle intense internal and external pressures (e.g. the pressure to bring in funding or to publish) to nurture and build relationships that provide fertile ground for partnership work. However, it is off the back of this work that many exemplar projects, those that have real impact, those that also form the backbone of university strategies, case studies and local stories, will come to bear fruit.

Note

1 *Civil society* can be understood as the 'third sector' of society, distinct from government and business and including the family and the private sphere.

Chapter 4

Change and university cultures

Introduction

This chapter outlines some of the next steps in creating, developing or supporting authentic learning approaches. Having considered the ways in which the university community can work with external partners in Chapter 3, we now turn our attention to how to work with internal stakeholders and how to navigate the murky world of university cultures and subcultures. In seeking to advance authentic learning, it's likely that we're engaging in versions of institutional and professional change, so the sections that follow are designed to offer a range of tactics that we can deploy in order to manage this process successfully and to support our continued development as academic or professional services staff.

The chapter provides an exploration of potential actions and strategies with relation to these themes:

1   Recognising the opportunities and barriers inherent within different university cultures
2   Understanding how to initiate authentic learning activity
3   Forming collaborations with others who can help, facilitate or fund
4   Understanding our contributions to broader change agendas
5   Recognising how authentic learning supports the development of new and sustainable forms of professional identity

We draw on the experiences of our collaborators, as well as contemporary texts and reports, to reflect on these issues, to offer informed and realistic alternatives for colleagues at different stages of their career and to construct the beginning of a pathway for institutions to follow more broadly. The chapter is therefore divided into these five sections:

1   Institutional cultures: closed or open systems?
2   The impact of disciplinary culture
3   Initiating authentic learning: practical steps

4   Professional identities
5   Components of a purposeful culture

To begin our journey, we consider the impact of institutional and disciplinary cultures on the ability to embed authentic learning approaches within
universities to encourage you to reflect on the culture in your workplace
and how this may enable, or constrain, your chances of successfully imple-
menting authentic learning. We're optimists about the value and relevance
of authentic learning as a pedagogy that transcends diverse universities and
academic disciplines. Yet we're also pragmatists and recognise that in some
universities and in some disciplines, this work may prove more problematic than in others. Yet we have faith in the power of individuals to trans-
form or manipulate dominant pedagogic practices and discourses in favour
of authentic learning approaches that in some institutions may be viewed
counter to the norm.

Institutional cultures: closed or open systems?

As educators operating within universities, we're shaped by our institutions,
by distinct institutional cultures that reveal underlying assumptions about
knowledge and learning and that shape our practices. Our professional
identities – whom we have 'permission' to be and what we have 'permission' to do – are shaped by our institutions but equally may shape them.
Of course, institutional cultures are mixed and complex, moulded not least
by fields and disciplinary communities that themselves are underpinned by
varying ideas about knowledge and learning. However, as we saw in Chapters 1 and 2, Martin (2012) helpfully delineates between two broad university 'species': the 'classical' and the 'technical.' In the former, knowledge
produced is conceived as 'pure' (that is, produced by and circulated within
disciplines), whilst in the latter, it is 'applied' (that is, produced within the
context of its application).

As Lounsbury and Pollack (2001) argue, these two species of university
represent two different logics concerning educational practices and assumptions about knowledge and learning therein. Closed-system logic is found
in classical universities. In this system, knowledge is constructed as universal and objective, with universities separate from broader social institutions
and processes, those 'ivory towers' whose very separateness from the world
allows them to make propositions about it.

Within closed systems, it is faculty[1] who have the legitimacy to produce knowledge (Butin, 2010), which they share through particular institutions such as journals, conferences, lectures and seminars. Pedagogic
practices seek to equip students with the ability to advance knowledge of
a subject in a disinterested, critical way (Bourner, 2010). Students exist
as empty vessels, topped up by faculty, the 'sages on the stage.' Learning

is therefore teacher centred, controlled and linear, the very antithesis of authentic learning.

With their fostering of connections between universities and wider society and their opening up to the wider world, authentic learning approaches typify the open-system logic prevalent in 'technical' species of university. Here, knowledge is particularistic and shaped by individual experiences, with learning student centred and controlled. Technical universities have grown in number and status with the expansion of higher education and have often focused on the need to improve teaching methods in order to successfully engage with larger and more diverse classes (Haggis, 2006). Faculty have become 'guides on the side', designing learning methods and environments that encourage innovation and teamwork. Despite the occasional disparaging attitudes of those in classical cultures, these methods don't lead to a loss of criticality. In some instances, they may well antagonise and critique relations between universities and society as much as endorse them.

Assumptions about knowledge and learning and associated faculty practices for closed- and open-system logics are summarised in Figure 4.1.

Closed-system logic ('classical' universities)	Open-system logic ('technical' universities)
Assumptions about knowledge and learning: • University as 'storehouse of knowledge' • Knowledge exists 'out there' • Knowledge comes in 'chunks' delivered by instructors • Learning is cumulative and linear • Learning is teacher centred and controlled • Classroom and learning are competitive and individualistic	Assumptions about knowledge and learning: • University as 'learning environment' • Knowledge is particularistic and shaped by individual experience • Knowledge is constructed and created • Learning is a nesting and interacting of frameworks • Learning is student centred and controlled • Learning environments are cooperative and supportive
Faculty practices: • Expert/disseminator of knowledge • Faculty are primarily lecturers • Faculty and students act independently and in isolation • Teachers classify and sort students • Any expert can teach	Faculty practices: • Innovator/facilitator • Faculty are primarily designers of learning methods, and environments and are encouraged to innovate • Faculty and students work as a team • Teachers develop every student's competencies and talents • Empowering learning is challenging and complex

Figure 4.1 Competing logics of university education (Lounsbury and Pollack, 2001: 324)

The differentiation between classical and technical species of university and associated closed- and open-system logics gives a useful point of reflection if we are to try to establish authentic learning approaches within our own institutions. It is not our contention that any one university will be purely 'classical' or purely 'technical.' In reality, complex blends will exist. However, we do contend that, within the United Kingdom, the classical – that culture maintaining disinterestedness, separateness from the world, impartiality and a 'freedom' and 'autonomy' to pursue the 'truth' – remains normative, for several political and historical reasons.

First, as Bourner (2010) argues, the transition from an elite to a mass higher education system in the United Kingdom happened at a relatively late stage of the country's economic development. The subsequent existence of a binary system of higher education into the 1990s saw many of the pressures to change higher education, including the drive for civic engagement, placed at the door of polytechnic universities rather than at research-intensive universities. It is these research-intensives that still dominate both national and international league tables and provide the benchmark to which others aspire.

Second, Naidoo and Jamieson (2006: 878) tender that universities may utilise their "high levels of academic, reputational and financial capital" to "engage in practices intent on conserving the academic principles structuring the field of education." Thus, classical academic culture endures as a stubborn inner core to the academic world, a core with which authentic learning must compete if it is to be legitimised.

The impact of disciplinary culture

As we've already intimated, institutional cultures are complex, shaped in part by disciplinary communities. As we look to implement authentic learning within our institutions, we may be more swayed by immediate disciplinary cultures than wider institutional ones, particularly if we're in academic roles. Just as faculty practices are influenced by systems that are broadly closed or open, so too may they be affected by varied cultures of learning across disciplines. Such cultures frame what staff and students expect to happen in a given learning setting and what they understand and value as 'knowledge' (Jin and Cortazzi, 2006). Undoubtedly, certain disciplinary cultures are more congruent with authentic learning approaches than others.

Butin (2010: 30) differentiates epistemological characteristics in disciplines across two spectra – 'hard/soft' and 'pure/applied' – as in Figure 4.2.

Whilst the previous distinctions are socially constructed monikers, we suggest that authentic learning approaches more naturally align with 'applied' disciplines, themselves indicative of open systems. This isn't to discount the potential role of 'pure' knowledge within authentic learning. The independence of pure knowledge, its freedom from context, means

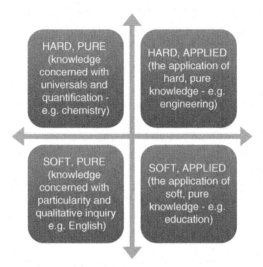

Figure 4.2 Differentiating spectra for academic disciplines

that it's portable – it can be utilised in different settings to generate new understanding and new solutions. Those with access to pure knowledge are, for Young and Muller (2013), most likely to be able to bring imagination into play and to envisage alternative approaches. In a 'real world' setting, pure knowledge can be used by students and external communities to view, analyse and address issues through new lenses. And in so doing, new light may be brought to bear on the pure knowledge itself. We therefore believe that authentic learning need not be the sole preserve of applied disciplines (especially those providing training for professional practice) but that pure disciplines also have much to contribute and to gain.

For those of us working in universities or departments where classical academic cultures prevail or in disciplines that reify pure knowledge, the challenge to legitimise authentic learning is real. As defined by Suchman (1995: 574, cited by Farrugia and Lane, 2012: 416):

> Legitimacy is a generalised perception or assumption that the actions of an entity are desirable, proper, or appropriate within some socially constructed system of norms, values, beliefs, and definitions.

Authentic learning approaches are counter-normative pedagogies, subordinate within classical culture and thus seeking legitimacy. To secure this legitimacy, we must identify those in whose gift it lies. Dependent on context, this could be directors of studies, heads of department or relevant professional services that support departments. We must then recognise and understand their conditions for conferring legitimacy (Farrugia and Lane, 2012). In other words, we need to work on our pitch, the 'hook' which will grab their attention and support. We may well need to 'play the game', couching our work or ideas in language that speaks to the dominant culture.

We don't want to suggest a 'one-size-fits-all' approach to a pitch that would secure legitimacy for authentic learning within classical or pure disciplinary cultures. However, we'd argue that any pitch should, in part, explain how the authentic learning approach will serve as an academic activity of equal value to more traditional academic activities, one rooted in critical discourse and reflection rather than in uncritical modes of doing. The opportunity to apply and critically review pure knowledge in its application is essential. In addition, approaches that emphasise service over learning, that appear explicitly ideological rather than critical, are unlikely to curry favour and legitimisation within a classical university. Dogma risks reducing universities to service agencies at the expense of their role as learning communities (Kezar and Rhoads, 2001).

As advocates of authentic learning within our institutions, we'll need to act as agents of change to secure the legitimisation of our desired pedagogic method. Securing such support will likely be easier if we're based in applied disciplines within wider institutions that exhibit open-systems logics. If we find ourselves positioned within pure disciplines and institutional cultures reifying closed-systems logics, we'll need to expend greater effort in convincing significant stakeholders of the academic value of our approach and ensure it's one that enables critical application of pure knowledge.

Initiating authentic learning: practical steps

Once we have an understanding of our context and likely reactions to pedagogical innovations, we can consider how our influence can be brought to bear. Clearly, this will be dependent to a great extent upon our particular role and responsibilities, but there are steps that every individual can take when they have access to the teaching realm. As soon as we have control of a class, a series of classes or learning episodes, or better still a unit or module as a whole, we can begin the process of opening up our work to external influences. Authentic learning experiences can be created without recourse to greater authorities and at relatively low risk, at the level of a single session. The further a process is extended, the more likely it is that negotiation will have to take place with other stakeholders, whether they're other staff contributing to the module in question, professional service colleagues or even the students themselves.

Ironically, it is in the classical systems that individual academics often have the greater capacity to impose a consistent pedagogical approach. This is because modules will often be organised around the research interests of a particular individual rather than the needs of a curriculum per se. Technical cultures tend to be more collaborative, with teaching teams and multiple contributors to modules more common. Introducing new interventions to these settings may require more conversations but conversely is more likely to generate support and lead to effective shared practice. In all settings, however, the stakes are raised as soon as we tangle with assessment. At this point, our work is likely to be subject to authorisation from others in a course team, formally or informally, and we'll start to find ourselves more regularly on the doorstep of institutional gatekeepers such as course or programme leaders, field chairs or directors of study.

In preparing a pitch for a new approach to module design or assessment, we recommend that you focus on potential benefits that will gain traction in your environment. In predominantly technical institutions, this may be straightforward, but in more classically inclined spaces, the approach will need to be more subtle. It may be possible to secure support and approval on the basis of educational arguments, for example, the proposition that students will develop their critical thinking skills more effectively in these settings, but often more secondary or instrumental motives may appear less threatening or controversial. In many of these environments, particular themes or approaches will be in vogue, for example, 'graduate employability' is a notion that has currency across the sector in the present climate. For many STEM subjects in the hard/pure and hard/applied quadrants of Butin's grid, professional accreditation and the approval of a professional or industry body are of increasing importance. Applied approaches that facilitate greater interaction with relevant organisations and settings play well with these stakeholders. There will be narratives that afford us opportunities to legitimise new approaches, but we'll need to listen and observe carefully and take time to understand the institutional climate and corporate priorities if we're to be successful in the long term.

In all settings, we recommend that you evidence and demonstrate your collaborations in order to support your pitch. These can be with your students, who in general (though not all cases) are likely to support a process that offers them greater agency and engagement (see Healey et al., 2014). They can be with internal partners, for example, library or learning services, outreach departments, civic engagement officers, skills teams or even representatives from central learning and teaching services, who are likely to welcome and support innovations. They will also, of course, be your external partners where these connections are central to the new provision. Demonstrating this support can positively impact the confidence of the gatekeeper, whose view of legitimacy may be swayed by the views of others in the institution. It will also help to make the case in relation to efficiency. While there might be some short-term investment of time and energy to establish any new approach, the presence and input of partners will, in time, ease the burden of delivery on the host department.

While the gatekeepers can constrain new approaches, many will be pro-tagonists themselves. Their role as local leaders may extend into the realms of line management, and they will certainly carry with them status, some influence and the potential to disrupt and rebuild notions of legitimacy. In all settings, gatekeepers and local leaders will be able to shape agendas, influence budgets, negotiate timetables and, crucially, oversee or lead curriculum development opportunities. In the short term, this last aspect will relate to low-level changes to modules in order to make them more applied or to support greater permeability. In the longer term, through reviews, validations and wider 'transformations', local leaders will be able to support the embedding, 'mainstreaming' and sustainability of authentic learning.

Fung's (2017) breakdown of the components of curriculum design is a useful starting point for considering how gatekeepers and local leaders can support authentic learning at the planning stage. The value of particular forms of learning can be communicated to students in a number of ways, including the status of modules (optional or compulsory), their position (single or double term or semester) and their weight or credit size. Their position in the degree will also be interpreted by students in various ways, for example, the difference between an 'introductory', 'core' or capstone, final module. While there will be considerations at the level of an individual module, to ensure coherence and credibility, there will also be potential connections between modules that can be developed. For example, to what extent are authentic learning experiences supported by activities in other modules? Are there opportunities to build relevant skills in preparation for research-engaged opportunities? Is authentic learning part of a coherent suite of learning activities that lead seamlessly to appropriate outcomes? These kinds of question will normally be answered by local learning and teaching strategies, and by addressing them carefully, leaders can ensure that authentic learning is integrated and not a vulnerable, disconnected, standalone activity.

Given that local leaders are likely to have extended experience in an institution, they are also well placed to offer guidance to individuals seeking to innovate, assisting them with appropriate networks, alerting them to developmental programmes and funding opportunities and advising them on wider organisational climate. Understanding how new approaches fit with broader institutional priorities and strategies is critical for long-term success, so connecting individuals to these stakeholders and agendas can be extremely helpful. At a basic human level, the most significant thing that a local leader can do is offer encouragement, tolerance and collaboration. Innovation will so often be derailed by cynicism or a lack of enthusiasm, but a local leader can do much to encourage, support and protect. Creating a positive motivational climate, in which colleagues have the right levels of 'psychological safety' to enable them to suggest new approaches and to see them through, can have a significant effect on behaviours and encourage the kind of risk-taking and collaboration that our case study contributors insist is essential for success.

In addition to influencing team or departmental cultures, local leaders can also positively impact the formation of teams. A great deal of academic life is organised around teams, but their creation is often accidental or arbitrary, and little thought is given to the factors underlying high performance or the kinds of contributions that might be required from individuals in order to achieve success. Consideration of these aspects could prove significant in taking authentic learning to the next level, through the creation of strong and effective collaborations and supportive connections, such as communities of practice or mentoring schemes.

Finally, local leaders have the capacity to influence recruitment and to encourage applications from individuals who can help advance the cause. Many university recruitment procedures are crude and fail to assess either pedagogical intent or collaborative capabilities, but these issues can be addressed and relevant processes improved. Job descriptions and adverts could help to communicate a departmental intent to focus on these approaches, and selection activities could include consideration of design issues or analysis of different forms of assessment. When we recruit and develop future academics, we do have choices. We can continue to reproduce the standard, 'traditional' lecturer, or we can consider more carefully the capabilities that are required by the individuals who can make contributions to authentic learning and build effective experiences and environments for students in the future. In so doing, we will be explicitly promoting new forms of professional identity, to which we now turn.

Professional identities

It is through our professional identities that we enact change. Professional identities encapsulate who we are and how we act – our 'beings' and 'doings' – within institutions. More than this, they indicate who we want to become (Clarke et al., 2013). Slay and Smith (2011: 87) define professional identity as "the constellation of attributes, beliefs, and values people use to define themselves in specialised, skill- and education-based occupations or vocations." With relation to authentic learning work, how we define, or wish to define, ourselves, and how we're defined by others, is therefore instructive. Billot (2010) suggests that identities arise from interactions between individuals and their contexts, between agency and structure. Over the following sections, we consider structure and agency in turn before surmising the impacts on authentic learning work.

Our workplaces matter, for they mould us, shaping our ways of thinking, feeling and doing and our understandings of what it means to 'be' a certain type of professional and the type of work and knowledge reified within any given field (Archer, 2008b; Burke et al., 2017; Ranson and Stewart, 1998).

According to Webb (2015), there are three main contextual workplace factors that shape professional identity:

1   *Distinctiveness:* How a profession's values and practices relate to other comparable groups;
2   *Prestige:* An emphasis on status, reputation and credentials. Success within a career is often associated with a successful professional identity construction;
3   *Salience of the out-group:* Awareness of the out-group, those who do not belong, reinforces awareness of in-group.

As we come to define and think of ourselves as authentic learning practitioners within universities, we consider what it is that makes us distinctive from other faculty and what success might look like. Professional identity work therefore also includes consideration of what it means to be 'unprofessional' (Webb, 2015), to 'fail' to be and act in a certain way. Indeed, institutions often strengthen 'in-groups' through powerful shaming devices of 'out-groups' as 'unprofessional.' We should take care to notice, then, who are the 'in-groups' within our universities that are reified as 'proper' professionals? And does authentic learning feature as an aspect of 'proper' professionalism, or are there aspects of it deemed 'unprofessional'?

Institutional and disciplinary cultures provide key contexts with which we interact, contexts that socialise us and that may either enable or constrain the implementation of authentic learning pedagogies. For academics, initial socialisation into the profession, normally via a PhD or related postgraduate qualification, can seem out of kilter with their experience of their first substantive post, often a fellowship or lectureship where other skills have greater prominence and value. Research and teaching are clearly related activities in university contexts, but they require different skillsets. Not every successful researcher will become a successful educator, and the idea that a PhD is helpful preparation for the vocation of a teacher is misleading, to say the least. Not every reluctant teacher can be successfully retrained or converted by a Postgraduate Certificate of Higher Education (PGCHE) or equivalent, and consequently many academics struggle to locate or position themselves within their new environment.

This is particularly the case in research-intensive universities, where prestige is likely associated with success in research activities and where classical orientations pertain. Indeed, both Henkel (2005) and Quigley (2011) note the primacy of discipline in academic working lives. Despite the shift in recent decades to applied research, making a distinctive academic contribution to a specific discipline remains foremost, as does academic freedom. This 'freedom' is conceived as autonomy to choose and pursue a research agenda over and above any particular teaching activities. When teaching does occur in research-intensives, traditional approaches likely predominate, with the locus of control centred on the academic and risk, flexibility and permeability minimised. The notion of the 'lecturer' as a job title is also significant here, reinforcing expectations of the form of delivery required and the nature of relationships between the academic and their stakeholders.

Over recent decades, the imperatives of global neoliberalism, imbued with discourses of 'competition' and 'excellence', have compelled academics towards identities for and of the market (Burke et al., 2017). Academics have been forced to acknowledge and develop other forms of capability. Becher and Trowler (op cit) argue that academics now need to engage with further 'scholarships' of leadership, management, administration and entrepreneurship. These demands have intensified in a period when universities have become increasingly managerialist and consumerist in orientation (Deem et al., 2007). The growth in new public managerialism within the 'corporate' university necessitates staff that are flexible, productive, resilient and oriented towards economic objectives (Archer, 2008a; Burke et al., 2017).

Within the corporate university, pressure exists to be the 'right' kind of academic producing the 'right' products. Archer (2008a: 389) contends that the products reified are "the winning of external revenues for research" and the production of 'high quality' publications as recognised through peer review processes. These 'outputs' are deemed important, as they contribute to "an institution's overall strategy to maintain and improve its market position" (Harriss, 2005: 426). Pressure to conform to, and master, modes of performativity leads to a fear of difference, to aversion to the forms of risk-taking and identity work that are integral to authentic learning approaches (Burke et al., 2017).

Another effect of managerialism has been increasing fragmentation and specialisation, particularly in relation to the 'bifurcation' of research and teaching; the growth of para-academic work such as skills development or research management (MacFarlane, 2010) and the associated increase in support or administrative 'professional service' roles. Although these new or revised roles indicate a diversification of activity within universities, we should not mistake this for an increase in diversity within the workforce itself. Despite the implication that universities are more open to external expertise than has previously been the case, they remain bastions of privilege and overwhelmingly employ able-bodied people from white, middle-class backgrounds (ECU, 2009).

In conforming to neoliberal values, identities and practices within the academy, academics are subject to a form of 'symbolic violence' (Burke et al., 2017). Those seen as different, who fail to conform to idealised sets of standards and homogenising practices that signify the likes of 'quality' and 'excellence', are often viewed as 'high-risk' and threatening to academic standards – the powerful shaming device of being 'unprofessional.' There is a risk that in some universities, authentic learning practitioners may fall prey to symbolic violence due to their 'non-traditional' approaches. However, to paint academics as powerless pawns in the face of managerialist discourses is to deny their undoubted ability to resist – their agency – to which we now turn.

None of us enter the workplace as empty vessels, devoid of our own morals and values and previous workplace knowledge, skills and experiences. We all carry distinctive histories. These influence how we approach our new professional context, making judgements as to what is 'good', 'bad' or 'important' (Fitzmaurice, 2013). As such, our agency shapes development of our professional identity as we subjectively assign meaning to the way we understand and approach work within our institutions.

Archer (2008a: 397) suggests that individual academics may construct their professional identity as "a form of 'principled' personal project", one underpinned by "core values of intellectual endeavour, criticality, ethics and professionalism." She contends that notions of happiness and self-fulfilment are more important to academics than instrumental measures of success, an emphasis on collegiality and collaboration above individualistic drive. Indeed, Fitzmaurice (2013) argues that moral purposefulness, beyond mere notions of performativity, is a key motivator for early career academics, who demonstrate a desire to serve others for the greater good of society.

Tension can therefore exist between collegiate, 'principled' projects and the competitive, individualistic practices currently on the ascendant within higher education. In response to these tensions, academics may actively 'unbecome' (Colley et al., 2007), resisting roles and identities imposed by the sector for those more congruent with their agency. The adoption of authentic learning identities may be positioned as 'unbecomings' by some academics, for they intimate new ways of thinking, working and being that challenge normative academic identities. Alternatively, Archer (2008b) argues that some academics perform a balancing act between their collegiate, 'principled' projects and the competitive, individualistic practices found within higher education. They achieve this through a psychic splitting between "performances of self and the internalised sense of self" (ibid: 282) in which they *do* without *being* a neoliberal subject. So, as we suggested in the previous section, advocates may look to 'sell' the approach using language and discourses that fit normative frames whilst their intentions remain counter-normative.

We've outlined a range of structural and agential influences that, through their interaction, have shaped the professional identities of academics and professional services staff operating in C21st UK universities. For those who operate in cultures that are overtly classical or corporate, care must be taken to ensure that their 'non-traditional' actions do not lead to their isolation or marginalisation. Many achieve this, successfully integrating authentic learning in their curriculum while avoiding elephant traps that might undermine their legitimacy. For those operating in more technical or applied environments, adopting new forms of professional identity will be a less hazardous process but equally worthy of care and consideration.

Components of a purposeful culture

Most of the current chapter has been prudent, identifying tactics and strategies for change but always wary of the detractors, mindful of those who seek to undermine. But there is a more optimistic way to look at the world, which considers what might encourage, facilitate and support. In this section, we explore the components of a purposeful culture, one where authentic learning is a core element of the normative culture and where colleagues act collectively and without cynicism to foster imagination and innovation.

A purposeful culture would, we think, be one where collaboration, openness and risk are all encouraged and embraced. Authentic learning requires universities to stimulate co-operation for teams of staff and students to find effective ways to partner with stakeholders beyond the traditional academic community. It requires agile and flexible provision – so courses and learners who can access opportunities quickly and efficiently – and it requires permeable borders – so physical and cultural spaces that allow knowledge and members of the academic community out and external stakeholders and their expertise in.

Working with others to enable authentic learning requires the academic community to relinquish control of the educational experience. In contrast to the traditional or classical mode, where the lecturer controls the dissemination and potential acquisition of knowledge and manages forms of assessment where the majority of outcomes are known, predictable and repeated year-on-year, authentic learning undermines certainties. With authentic learning, authority is shared more widely, students become more active, outcomes are less predictable and each year brings new challenges and different results. In other words, an engaged culture will take more risks. It will have to offer greater trust, empower others by allowing them greater say and agency and be willing for things to go wrong. It will have to be what Grint (2010) describes as 'risk-enabled', supporting an environment that values people and collaboration, is empowering and gives a clear sense of direction and purpose for the organisation as a whole. This culture will encourage and accept risk, seek new and imaginative approaches, value open feedback and be sufficiently malleable and informal to accept positive change at any level.

These ideas are reflected in Mason O'Connor et al.'s (2011: 39) vision of a 'facilitative environment' for pedagogical approaches which seek to engage local and regional communities. Here, a "structural openness to external influence through the research agenda and the curriculum" is encouraged, as is a "willingness to adopt a shared agenda and mutually beneficial collaborations." The importance of institutional co-ordination and planning is also highlighted, alongside the need for effective planning and an approach to budgeting that recognises the value of engaged learning. In other words, a facilitative environment is one where any new forms of costs are acknowledged and covered. It is also somewhere that makes obvious statements about the value of innovation, through celebrations and promotional events and literature and via reward structures including promotion criteria, institutional awards, funding and fellowships.

Institutions can make clear their commitment to different forms of learning through their public pronouncements and policies. Corporate plans and learning and teaching strategies will emphasise different and preferred approaches, but of course there may be some distance between corporate documents and the 'lived experience' at any institution. More subtle indicators of priorities are the messages that dominate websites or social media outlets and the images that are prevalent on campus. Messages are, of course, reflected by other forms of cultural reproduction, including the kinds of people who are employed and the forms of expertise that are valued at times of promotions or the granting of chairs or professorships. An engaged university would use these forms of messaging to give confidence to those who seek to innovate and encourage others to offer support, patience and praise where necessary. One persistent impediment to change is the jealousy of the next-door neighbour, who may be threatened by change and seek to undermine it through covert criticism or behind-the-scenes networking. A risk-enabled team would be one that encouraged innovation and stood shoulder to shoulder when things failed to go according to plan, offering praise wherever due.

However, cultural 'enablers' may be of limited value if the structures of the institution are insufficiently flexible to support change. Getting authentic learning right means being able to react quickly to opportunities, to change schedules or to adapt assessments. Course and module documentation therefore must be open to sensible and speedy change, with control resting at the hands or desks of the academics rather than an unwieldy system that takes months or even years to say 'yes.' Anxiety around these issues has increased in recent years, thanks largely to legislation on consumer protection, but appropriate levels of flexibility are possible within most current institutional frameworks if learning outcomes are written with the right skill and generosity.

Understanding how to manage these processes leads us to the last critical component of an engaged institution – the availability of appropriate training and educational opportunities and resources for those staff who wish to engage in authentic learning but who lack the craft knowledge and/or the confidence to do so. These opportunities must be embedded in all forms of training and acculturation, from induction programmes to introductory or probationary courses to stand-alone qualifications. Where this emphasis is reflected in mentoring or coaching schemes, and is manifested in communities of practice, the chances of success will be even greater.

Conclusion

In this chapter, we've demonstrated that academic staff at all institutions have the capacity to initiate and sustain authentic learning. This capacity will vary according to their career stage and also the various environmental factors that support or constrain innovation. Success will be dependent, to a great extent, on the ability of the individual to 'read' their local and institutional cultures and to adopt pitches and approaches that are cognisant of these influences. These individuals will also need to be willing to embark on journeys where their professional identity may be more fluid than they had originally anticipated and where they may have to present particular 'faces' at different times in order to maintain their progress and their position.

Authentic learning is new to many departments and faculties. It'll be experienced as 'change' and therefore resisted by many. However, our case studies indicate that resistance can often be overcome and that authentic learning can become embedded at institutions of all ages, locations and emphases. We have used this chapter to suggest approaches and strategies that can be employed by colleagues in the pursuit of change, but ultimately much of what will be achieved in the future will be down to your own willingness to put your head above the parapet and to grasp the moment to do things differently.

Note

1 By 'faculty', we mean permanent or 'tenured' academic staff with the contractual and cultural capability to conduct research.

Chapter 5

Global perspectives

Introduction

In this chapter, we take a brief and cursory look at authentic learning through a global lens. Or, at the very least, we leave the shores of the United Kingdom for a short while. It is such a broad area for exploration that what we cover here is merely the tip of the iceberg. We promised at the outset of this book that we would not get too hooked into definitions and terminology of authentic learning but would work with a broad-church definition and bring together a kaleidoscope of distinct but related approaches. With this spirit, we take a look at how policy agendas and societal needs have shaped authentic learning in cultures outside of the United Kingdom.

We begin by looking at five contrasting nation states in the Global North (the United States and Canada) and the Global South (chiefly India, but with insights from Brazil and South Africa). We then turn our focus to the role that authentic learning plays in conflict societies, in response to natural disasters and within truth and reconciliation work. The purpose of this chapter is to lay way-markers for practices and ideas that we can learn from here in the United Kingdom, to surface the key terminology and ideas used in these contexts and to point the way to further exploration. Without any further ado, let us set off on our travels.

The Global North (United States and Canada: community engaged and service learning)

In service learning, students learn and develop academic knowledge, skills and personal attributes through tackling real-life problems in their community. We find, too, that there is no one thing called service learning; it takes many forms. It can be viewed as consisting of multiple, divergent modes of practice often contradictory but overall, a broad church consisting of learning through doing social good (Butin, 2010). Some researchers have tried to break down the approaches into a set of typologies. For example, Sigmon (1994) identified approaches which emphasise the service element (i.e. helping the community) over the learning, others that focus more on the learning scaffolded through community engagement and, finally, those where the learning and the service are finally balanced. Andrew Furco, another key actor in the institutionalising of service learning across US education, argues that typologies and classifications play a useful role in helping both insiders and outsiders share understandings of what is being discussed. For many proponents of service learning, it is the balance and mutual reinforcement of learning goals and service goals that form the cornerstone of the practice. Service learning differs from internship, placement experience or volunteer work in its "intention to equally benefit the provider and the recipient of the service as well as to ensure equal focus on both the service being provided and the learning that is occurring" (Furco, 1996). It is important, too, to acknowledge that when practitioners refer to learning, they don't just refer to learning about course content but a broader appreciation of the discipline and an enhanced sense of personal values and civic responsibility.

The term was coined in the 1970s but has its roots in the early 1900s. John Dewey (1916) is often credited with providing the theoretical and pedagogical pillars of service learning. His key ideas include democracy as a way of life, where everybody has to participate in order to bring democratic values to life, the idea of learning from experience through doing and linking educational establishments to the community. In a departure from traditional educators that stressed the 'sage on the stage', rote learning and the authoritarian teacher, Dewey emphasised *learning by doing* alongside community and democracy. In his book *The School and the Community*, Dewey wrote:

> When the school introduces and trains each child of society into membership within such a little community, saturating him with the spirit of service, and providing him with instruments of effective self-direction, we shall have the deepest and best guarantee of a larger society which is worthy, lovely and harmonious.

Dewey's ideas gave further flavour to the culture of many of the institutions established in the United States during the 1800s, many of which were established with a specific remit to engage communities and educate citizens, otherwise known as 'land grant' institutions.

Perhaps one of the most remarkable things about service learning in North America today is its ubiquity. In the United States, for example, in 2016, more than 450 higher education institutions reaffirmed their dedication to preparing students for engaged citizenship, to changing social and economic inequalities and to contributing to their communities as place-based institutions by signing Compact's 30th Anniversary Action Statement. Service learning is widely accepted as a key pedagogic approach through which many institutions will meet such aims, offering students real world learning experiences whilst meeting the needs of local communities.

Many universities in North America have established infrastructure to manage service learning programmes, enrich curriculum and support civic leadership in communities and amongst students. For example, there is the University of Chicago's Civic Engagement department (https://civicengage ment.uchicago.edu). At the time of writing, they have some 30 staff dedicated to working across research, teaching, civic engagement and innovation. Programmes such as the community accelerator, which develop capacity in local non-profit organisations, or UChicago local, which utilises the university's buying power for local benefit. Whilst neither is directly service learning per se, they build and create capacity within communities and create the conditions whereby service learning efforts can take root and flourish.

Another example is the University of British Columbia Learning Exchange (https://learningexchange.ubc.ca). Established in 1999, it runs a number of opportunities for experiential learning and community involvement whilst also welcoming the community into the university and developing curricula built on their experience and expert knowledge. As a practice which has largely become institutionalised within higher education and also secondary education, service learning is supported by a range of networks such as the International Association for Research on Service Learning and Community Engagement, and there are established national frameworks in place for measurement and classification, most notably the Carnegie Classification for Community Engagement.

The Global South (India, Brazil and South Africa)

Whilst Dewey was an influential thinker of his time, he wasn't alone. In other regions of the globe, there were people who extended his ideas. Paulo Freire, author of *Pedagogy of the Oppressed* (1970), for example, turned mainstream pedagogy on its head by insisting that true knowledge and expertise already exist within people. Starting out as a lawyer before turning to education and eventually becoming the director of the Department for Education and Culture in Brazil, he argued that education either functions as an instrument to indoctrinate people into the logic of the present system or becomes the practice of freedom in which people can deal critically and creatively with reality and discover how to participate in the transformation of their world. In this manner, his thinking was far more radical than Dewey, whose writing was arguably blind to issues of power and marginalisation.

India: community-based research

At 1.3 billion people, India is the second most populous country in the world. Its universities can be categorised into three main groups: government institutions, private aided institutions and private unaided institutions (Watson et al., 2011). The sector is overseen by the University Grants Commission (UGC), a statutory organisation of the government (www.ugc.ac.in). The UGC has had a longstanding interest in promoting (through funding) continuing adult education, extension and field outreach in a number of areas, including community harmony and peace education, human rights, environmental issues, health, women's empowerment and other social issues.

The UNESCO Chair in Community Based Research & Social Responsibility in Higher Education provides an invaluable resource into authentic learning practices in India. The chair is co-located between the University of Victoria (UVic) and the Society for Participatory Research in Asia (PRIA), whose head office is based in India. Writing about teaching and learning in India higher education, Wafa Singh (the India research coordinator of the UNESCO Chair in Community Based Research & Social Responsibility in Higher Education) states that India suffers from an outdated curriculum and models of course delivery and an absence of real world learning (Sing, 2018). Nevertheless, her report points to numerous examples of innovative practice where, through new courses, students can apply local knowledge and work to construct real world solutions.

Noteworthy examples from her report include:

- Courses on rural microfinance practices, folk medicine and so on. Developed by the Centre for Society University Interface and Research (CSUIR), these are largely relevant to the local rural society of Haryana.
- A scheme under which each college of the University of Pune adopts a village. Students from various disciplines are mandated to solve one particular need of the village they adopt. Examples include geography students using a geographic information system (GIS) to map the locality, history students documenting local history and chemistry students undertaking water/soil testing of the land.
- Courses on community-based participatory research (CBPR) in partnership with PRIA's International Academy (PIA). Through this approach, students undertake research with communities on topics of local importance.

(Sing, 2018)

A number of higher education institutions within India are influenced by the ideals and teachings of Mahatma Gandhi (Watson et al., 2011). His concept of *nai talim* directly relates to the delivery of what we call authentic learning. The concept is the idea that mental and manual work are necessarily connected and that work and knowledge are organically linked. Arguably, Gandhi's thinking on education goes much further and links theories of authentic learning more explicitly with social justice. For example, another of his relevant concepts is *sarvodaya* – the concept of lifting up all people in society. *Swaraj* is the concept of self-rule coming from the Independence movement and can be used as an expression of decolonisation of knowledge in higher education. And, finally, *jai jagat* is the concept of collective commitment to all life forms on the planet (Hall, 2019).

South Africa: community engagement

Since the end of apartheid, higher education reform in South Africa has focused on community engagement. In 1997, the White Paper on Higher Education affirmed as a priority the requirement that public higher education institutions 'demonstrate social responsibility and their commitment to the common good by making available expertise and infrastructure for community service programmes' (Favish, 2009). In 2004, the Higher Education Quality Committee identified 'knowledge-based community service' alongside research and teaching as the basis for accreditation and quality assurance (Watson et al., 2011). The general objective was to 'promote and develop social responsibility and awareness amongst students of the role of higher education in social and economic development through community service programmes' (Favish, 2009).

In response, universities across South Africa have established community engagement offices, at different stages of evolution in terms of embedding authentic learning opportunities in the curriculum. In their book *Engaged University: International Perspectives on Civic Engagement*, Watson et al. (2011) highlight practices from Cape Peninsula University of Technology which resonate with many of the case studies provided in this text. For example:

- Students in textiles work with low-income women in the townships to teach them how to design and produce clothing for specific occupations.
- Students in radiology support community health clinics and produce health awareness posters as part of their degree.
- Students in chemistry work with local schools to inspire and engage young people in science.

(Watson et al., 2011; Hall, 2009)

Authentic learning in responsive mode: from natural disasters to conflict

Education is often lauded for its role in building community and contributing to cohesion in society. Universities can have a tendency to proclaim themselves benign actors in social drama, focusing on liberation and empowerment, without necessarily considering exclusion and power. The Truth and Reconciliation work in North America and Australia has begun to awaken universities to the notion that for many Indigenous people, 'education' was a form of repression and abuse. It was intended to destroy cultures and fracture communities. The effects of this 'education' are still playing out today in broken lives and shattered families (Truth and Reconciliation, 2015).

Education can fuel conflict. It can do this by reinforcing cohesion within groups to the exclusion of the 'other.' For example, higher-level education may grant access to further rights, resources and benefits (e.g. higher pay, increased life expectancy), and yet access to such rights is determined by race, class, ethnicity and so on. Education can also maintain societal norms and values, usually those of the dominant group or culture. In doing so, it has the potential to fuel grievances and separation through socialisation and identity development and has as much potential to do this as it does of mediating or healing them (Bush and Saltarelli, 2000; Obura, 2003; Millican, 2017).

There are, however, profound reasons education must teach us more than knowledge but also how to use and apply knowledge ethically. In their chapter looking at the role of higher education in Israel, Owen et al. (2018) point to a letter written by a teacher, psychologist and Holocaust survivor, who calls upon other teachers not just to promote knowledge but to develop our collective humanity:

> Dear Teacher:
> I am a survivor of a concentration camp. My eyes saw what no man should witness:
> Gas chambers built by learned engineers.
> Children poisoned by educated physicians.
> Infants killed by trained nurses.
> Women and babies shot and burned by high school and college graduates.
> So, I am suspicious of education.
> My request is: Help your students become human.
> (Ginott, 1972)

Education is therefore of central importance to creating societies in which individuals value the humanity and rights of others (Fung, 2017). There are examples where authentic learning or versions of this work contribute to transformations within post-conflict societies. Juliet Millican's (2017) edited collection *Universities and Conflict: The Role of Higher Education in Peacebuilding and Resistance* presents a number of case studies from around the world, including:

- Al-Quds Human Rights Clinic in Occupied Palestine. The clinic provides students with first-hand practical experience, enabling them to gain a well-rounded understanding of law towards promoting awareness of

international human rights and humanitarian law among the wider Palestinian society
- The Balkan Masters Programme. Developed in response to the conflict, the programme aimed to advance local peacebuilding and developed targeted exchanges and reflective learning across different nation states affected by the conflict.
- The responses from students in Myanmar to self-educate outside a crippled state system.

One final area to look at is the role of authentic learning in response to natural or humanitarian disasters. Whereas the curriculum-related work of universities in conflict areas may take place and evolve over years or decades, disasters require an immediate response. Typically, a university response may be led by groups of individuals working outside of the formal structures of the institution. Such was the case for the University of Canterbury in Christchurch, New Zealand, following the earthquakes of 2010 and 2011 which resulted in the deaths of over 400 people and significant destruction to the city's infrastructure. The response to this disaster initially came via the student body through the Student Volunteer Army which formed via Facebook shortly after the second quake. Subsequently, the university established a new course around the volunteer action. The *CHCH 101 Rebuilding Christchurch: An Introduction to Community Engagement in Tertiary Studies* course provides students with the opportunity to contribute to the recovery whilst also thinking critically about their efforts. The formal course also offers a long-term commitment to the recovery of the region (University of Canterbury, 2020). Also notable, although this returns us to the United Kingdom, is the response from King's College London to the Ebola outbreak (King's College London, 2018).

Conclusion

In this chapter, we've looked at authentic learning through the lens of different countries, cultures and societal needs. Our look at five different nation states has highlighted how the different traditions and institutional arrangements for higher education can affect how authentic learning takes place. And through looking at how universities might respond to different contexts, in particular those of conflicts and natural disasters, we've hopefully shed light on authentic learning in response mode. In each case, it is clear that there is real potential for authentic learning to contribute to, and shape, our experience as educators and learners, whether this be through developing new skills to support an emerging economy, through changing attitudes and behaviours or through changing social relations between groups dealing with the legacies of conflict and disaster.

Chapter 6

The case studies

We hope that you enjoy the 22 case studies that follow. We weren't aiming for a particular number; we just kept going until we ran out of time and didn't want to exclude any of those that we felt would be of interest. Each of the cases is presented in a format that enables you to understand the pedagogical tradition that has shaped the intervention, as well as how the approach is manifested at the particular institution on which we focus. We hope this gives you a flavour of the practicalities involved and also helps you to assess whether the approach might be adapted for use in your subject area.

In each instance, we give you an indication of institutions that favour the approach, as well as key references to enable you to pursue ideas further. We consider forms of assessment, likely 'levels' of study and positioning within curricula. The case studies are not, however, in a particular order – we haven't attempted to create themes or categories – because we want you to read through them all. We fear that by grouping, for example, all the 'business-related' cases together, it might discourage some readers from enjoying the full range of approaches and, in turn, prevent the imaginative application of pedagogies to new fields and subject areas. The only exception to this is the approach that we've described as 'service learning', where two closely related variants are presented together for ease of comparison.

There are some themes or emphases that run through several of the cases. Some of these relate to the nature of the partnerships involved in order to make them happen – some of these will be internal, some external, and there'll be variation on the reliance placed on other stakeholders. More fundamentally, the educative purpose of the cases will vary in often quite subtle ways. We identified in Chapter 2 the range of possible outcomes that underpin courses, modules and units, and this is reflected in the case studies, with some making explicit their commitment to the development of transferable skills and employability and others making clear their allegiance to social justice or equity. In some instances, the cases are about the practice of the discipline or professional field and enabling students to cut their teeth or begin their vocational journey.

A useful distinction to bear in mind is the notion is between students with their 'disciplinary coats' on and those with their coats off. If we take the example of a medical field like dentistry, it can be difficult to find ways to enable students to have their 'coats' on and to develop their practice in the field, in real world settings, from the start of their educational career. Sending first-years straight into clinical or surgical situations is challenging, and you're probably already finding the thought of this mildly alarming. However, there may be situations in which the students could use 'authentic' settings to develop contributory skills or bodies of knowledge, for example, in relation to listening skills or cultural awareness. To do this, it may be that the students take their 'coats off' in order to understand new settings or to develop skillsets that they later rely on in more conventional settings.

A final point of clarification is that we have not explored the realm of work-based learning or apprenticeships or any of those scenarios where the 'learning home' of a student is a workplace or a community setting. Our interest is in how conventional higher education, with the student located primarily in the university, connects with other realms or domains rather than those where students are 'released', in various ways, from a host setting to spend time with other students. We leave these approaches for others to explore.

1 Legal clinics

Related to

5 Science shops
11 Consultancy and client-led briefs
7 Business clinics

In the field

University of Hull
Cardiff University
King's College London

Typical assessment

Case study
Guidance documents
Reflective practice

Further reading

Kemp, V, Munk, T & Gower, S (2016) *Clinical Legal Education and Experiential Learning: Looking to the Future.* Manchester: University of Manchester, School of Law
Public Law Project (2018) *Public Law and Clinical Legal Environments: A Report on the Role of University Law Clinics in Increasing Access to Justice in Public Law, and the Role of Non-Governmental Organisations.* London: Public Law Project

Summary

Legal clinics bring together members of the public who require forms of legal advice with law students who work in supervised 'clinical' settings to offer guidance from their studies. The students are normally supervised by academic staff, who will be practising, certified solicitors and who will help to shape and validate the advice offered. Undergraduate and postgraduate students in law schools therefore have the opportunity to take part in hands-on legal work for the benefit of the wider community.

The clinics themselves can be housed in dedicated facilities, in some cases purpose-built and on campus, or can be in shared spaces on or off campus. Clinics offer advice that reflects the particular specialisms of the school or department concerned and advertise this expertise to the public. Clients bring their issue or question to the clinic, where students interview them and follow up with written advice gleaned from research or interaction with staff. The interests of all parties are protected by appropriate supervision, and clinics can operate with students from both undergraduate and post-graduate realms.

Our example comes from Hull University, which has operated a legal clinic since 2011. In October 2019, the clinic celebrated managing its 1,000th case and is a popular option for students in the third year of their LLB law degree. Members of the public request support from the clinic through the university's website and are then assigned an interview with two students, who use the interview to clarify their needs and requirements and then follow up with written guidance, normally in the realms of housing, employment, family or crime. Feedback from the public for this service has been overwhelmingly positive and has been welcomed by many given the relative lack of free legal advice available to the public in the city more widely.

Students at Hull are prepared for their work at the clinic through a two-week training programme which guides them in interview skills, how to construct and deliver advice, reflective practice and General Data Protection Regulation (GDPR) awareness. They are then placed in pairs in the clinic and host interviews with clients once a fortnight over a ten-week period. The interviews enable the students to fully understand the issues facing the client and are 'fact-finding' in nature. Advice and guidance aren't offered at this stage. The students have a post-interview debrief with a member of the academic staff and then begin a process of research that will inform their guidance. The students construct a letter to the client, which constitutes the legal advice, and this will contain detailed and thorough guidance as well as sources of additional information. The letter is approved by a member of staff and then sent to the client within two weeks of the original interview. This process gives students authentic experience of legal practice and enables them to develop professional skills while engaging with core issues in their discipline.

Assessment at Hull focuses on two aspects. First, students are introduced to models of reflective practice and are encouraged to develop a reflective log. A summary and analysis of this process forms one part of the assessment for the module and enables students to consider the challenges they faced as well as their interactions with clients, partners and staff. The other element of assessment is a case study, where a particular set of client needs are considered in more detail, advice is deconstructed and evaluated and direct connections made to academic bodies of knowledge. Although some aspects of clinical delivery are necessarily constrained, the assessments allow students greater freedom to explore and consider alternative approaches and interpretations.

The clinic is popular with all stakeholder groups. Members of the public offer consistently positive feedback through a client questionnaire, students enjoy and recognise the value of 'learning by doing' and staff consider the clinic 'the best parts of being in practice but without the interaction with clients.' Employers in the legal sector place a high value on clinical experience and, as a result, student demand for the clinic is high. Demand is currently managed through a competitive process where students apply to the module in the first instance.

The success of the Hull clinic is mirrored at many other institutions, although some choose to operate in the co-curricula realm and rely on voluntary effort from students and, in some cases, from staff. Depending on the availability of resources within a school, the range of legal services could be extended to representation. This could also be facilitated with external legal partners, who can and do support clinics in other ways. Legal clinics could potentially co-exist with other services to local or regional communities, for example, with social work students offering guidance on welfare issues, business or accounting students advising on financial matters and health or sport students supporting individuals with lifestyle decisions.

2 Public engagement

Related to

3 'Traditional' and 4 'critical' service learning
6 Event management
5 Science shops

In the field

University of Bath
University College London
Imperial College

Typical assessment

Literature reviews
Posters
Reflective practice

Further reading

Owen, D & Hill, S (2011) *Embedding Public Engagement in the Curriculum: A Framework for the Assessment of Student Learning from Public Engagement.* Bristol: National Co-ordinating Centre for Public Engagement
Varner, J (2014) Scientific outreach: Toward effective public engagement with biological science. *BioScience*, 64(4), pp 333–340

Summary

Public engagement is an agenda of increasing importance for universities. As institutions move further out of the shadows and into the public light, there's an expectation that they'll work hard to communicate the knowledge generated by their members to the wide range of stakeholders with an interest in science in its broadest forms. Engaging in effective two-way communication with a variety of 'publics' – including industry, policymaking institutions, education and local and regional communities – is essential if universities are to be seen as transparent, accountable and trusted organisations and if research and teaching are to be enhanced by incorporating the knowledges, experiences and perspectives from wider society. As a consequence, public engagement and the associated concept of research impact have enjoyed a high profile in recent Research Excellence Frameworks but also relate directly to one of the three fundamental purposes of the university that we explored in Chapter 1.

Best practice in this field is promoted by the National Coordinating Centre for Public Engagement, which emphasises the importance of mutuality in the relationships between universities and their partner agencies and communities. Academics will use a wide variety of means to foster effective engagement, from outreach and promotional events to collaborations with clients and patients, and from participatory arts to citizen science initiatives and more. A range of media will also be deployed to enhance communications, including more contemporary applications such as blogs, vlogs, digital stories and online resources. All of these initiatives to engage wider publics with cutting-edge research can be led and managed by academics, but they can also involve students at all levels of activity – from design to delivery to evaluation.

Public engagement with research commonly differentiates between three purposes for public engagement activity, either to inform (disseminate), consult or collaborate. These purposes can be used to categorise types of activity embedded into curricula where there's a strong bias towards 'informing' types. In these, teams of students may work with established academics to communicate key aspects of departmental or institutional research to targeted publics.

At the University of Bath, undergraduate modules have been developed by three departments in the faculty of science – physics, chemistry and pharmacy and pharmacology. Building on established good practice in the field of school outreach but driven by the desire to reach publics beyond the classroom, academic staff engage final-year students in designing public engagement activities to communicate current departmental research. While the projects have the benefit of realising departmental objectives, they also help staff to find a solution to the long-standing challenge of delivering transferable skills to students in STEM subjects. Public engagement enables those students who aspire to careers in fields beyond their core discipline to develop skills of value beyond the academy. However, it also maintains the integrity of the discipline in the sense that the students continue to engage with the core knowledge on the course – students have to be able to understand the research in order to communicate it effectively.

The Bath approach begins with a series of workshops that prepare students for the various phases of work that they'll have to manage in order to design and deliver a public engagement activity. These cover project management, team working, public engagement principles, evaluation techniques and reflective practice. Students then form small groups and are set two public engagement tasks, one to deliver an aspect of the university's research at an established science festival known as Bath Taps and the other to develop a novel activity for a partner agency. Students have engaged with a wide range of partners in order to achieve the second objective, including museums, aquariums, hospitals, visitor centres and science centres. In addition to devising and delivering a unique event, students have to liaise directly with the external agencies at all stages of the intervention. Students consistently deliver high-quality engagement activities that are appreciated by the host agencies and their publics. Feedback from all stakeholders is high, and students appreciate the opportunity to develop valuable skills that otherwise have a low profile within their degree.

Students at Bath are assessed in a variety of ways. Their initial grasp of departmental research is tested through a literature review. They then submit an activity brief, preceded by a 'pitch' to staff and peers. A reflective portfolio captures their learning from the intervention itself, and these different elements are synthesised in a viva which completes the module. This range of assessments can be usefully deployed where, as is the case at Bath, the modules run throughout the academic year. Shorter iterations might require more focused or streamlined assessments.

Collaborations between different departments at Bath demonstrate that public engagement can be embedded in many fields and disciplines. Staff share a core approach and a toolkit that guides workshops and supports high-quality delivery. There's also the possibility of interdisciplinary projects or even simple collaborations between departments where students come together to share practice or showcase their work. Established staff and research students can also be involved in various ways, either by helping to communicate their own findings or by offering mentoring or coaching support to student groups.

3 'Traditional' service learning

Related to

4 'Critical' service learning
15 Placements
11 Consultancy and client-led briefs

In the field

University of Warwick
King's College London
Newcastle University

Typical assessment

Reflective practice
Written report

Further reading

Annette, J (2010) The challenge of developing civic engagement in higher education in England. *British Journal of Educational Studies*, 58(4), pp 451–463
Deeley, S (2014) *Critical Perspectives on Service Learning in Higher Education*. Basingstoke: Palgrave Macmillan

See also

Details on the University of Warwick's Adopt-a-Class project: https://warwick.ac.uk/fac/arts/modernlanguages/intranet/undergraduate/yearabroad/yearabroad/aac/

Summary

As we introduced in Chapter 2, service learning has a long history, particularly within the North American context, but it's only in recent years that it's been adopted by a growing number of UK higher education institutions. As a pedagogic approach, service learning entails students working in partnership with local communities on service activities through structured programmes that include reflection. Service learning is therefore a three-pronged approach combining classroom learning, service activities and critical reflection.

The balance between these aspects shapes goals. Those programmes that emphasise change experienced by students – that is, learning – tend to the apolitical. They're the most prevalent in UK higher education settings and may be termed 'traditional.' Here, service outcomes are secondary and there's little, if any, critical exploration of the root causes of the service, of why it's needed.

Our case study of 'traditional' service learning is drawn from a modern languages undergraduate degree at the University of Warwick. Adopt-a-Class provides an opportunity for around eight third-year undergraduate students on Year Abroad placements in schools or partner universities in France, Germany or Spain to gather and/or create authentic foreign-language resources (e.g. museum leaflets, news articles, video clips, images, podcasts, PowerPoint presentations etc.) to share with primary or secondary school classes back in the United Kingdom.

The idea for Adopt-a-Class developed about ten years ago through the chief desire to motivate pupils in UK schools to aspire to modern languages study, providing a service of getting authentic foreign language resources into schools. The programme has evolved two aims – sharing the excitement of studying other languages and cultures through partnerships between schools and university students and the creation and curation of resources for Key Stages 3, 4 and 5.

For the Year Abroad students, the programme enables their sharing of their own passion for modern languages whilst developing an enhanced understanding of what it's like for UK-based pupils who have had limited intercultural experiences; it permits them to perceive issues through an alternative frame. It also encourages them to gather cultural observations of the foreign contexts in which they're placed. The programme convenor has noted that over the years, some of the Year Abroad students have chosen to partner with their old schools, the programme acting as an opportunity for them to 'give back.'

Prior to starting their placements, the Year Abroad students meet with a teacher in their chosen UK school and co-create a project plan, deciding such things as what authentic resources are required for when and how they'll be shared (some students arrange Skype sessions, record videos, write online reflections or simply post hard copies of resources). Ideas for potential classroom activities are also developed. Where students are working as language assistants in foreign schools, these schools are advised of Adopt-a-Class through a pro-forma letter but otherwise don't have a role to play.

As part of their Year Abroad placement, students must complete a reflective questionnaire which enables them to focus on, and articulate, the personal and professional development they have accrued, and here, they have an opportunity to reflect directly on Adopt-a-Class. Some students are teachers in the making, so the programme informs their future employability; a strong link with Warwick's Centre for Teacher Education has helped grow awareness of Adopt-a-Class further. The programme convenor has occasionally taken students along to academic conferences to present on their experiences, a way of enhancing their confidence and critical reflection further.

In addition to Adopt-a-Class, Year Abroad students undertake an assignment in which they create resources for Key Stage 3, 4 or 5 pupils that capture and present cultural diversity in creative and interactive ways. Modern languages teachers in UK schools then help refine ideas and shape resources so that they can be used directly within the classroom. Teachers have noted the added value of Year Abroad students as 'near-peers' to pupils' educational experiences. Pupils benefit from the personal stories and experiences of those relatively closer to their age than many teachers.

Challenges of the programme chiefly arise from the potential of sporadic communication between teachers and Year Abroad students once the school year has started. The requirement to co-create a project plan for the year upfront somewhat mitigates this. There's the risk of teachers moving on or of students not fulfilling the project plan as initially envisaged, so managing expectations up front through a clear introductory presentation is important, alongside administrative support to keep things on track.

Whilst the programme cannot be conceived as a piece of 'critical' service learning – it doesn't aim to address the structural inequalities or injustices that may have led to a decline in modern languages learning in UK schools and a dearth of authentic foreign language resources – it no doubt provides a valuable learning opportunity for the students involved and enables them to offer a service of inspiring the next generation of modern languages learners.

4 'Critical' service learning

Related to

3 'Traditional' service learning
22 Student action
5 Science shops

In the field

Nottingham Trent University
University of Brighton
King's College London

Typical assessment

Reflective practice
Written report
Poster

Further reading

Butin, D W (2010) *Service-Learning in Theory and Practice: The Future of Community Engagement in Higher Education*. Basingstoke: Palgrave Macmillan.
Mitchell, T D (2008) Traditional vs. critical service-learning: Engaging the literature to differentiate two models. *Michigan Journal of Community Service Learning*, Spring, pp 50–65

Summary

In Case Study 3, we presented an example of 'traditional' service learning, that which tends to the apolitical and emphasises the change experienced by students. Conversely, 'critical' service learning stresses change within both the community and student. It's therefore explicitly political and social justice oriented and possesses a focus on critical reflection that enables both students and communities to act as agents of change.

Many advocates of 'critical' service learning are inspired by the ideas and ideals expressed in Paolo Freire's (1970) seminal work, *Pedagogy of the Oppressed*, that focus on activating the critical consciousness of marginalised communities so that they may rise up and challenge oppressive forces within society. According to Mitchell (2008), three core orientations distinguish 'critical' service learning – a social change orientation, active work to address power imbalances and the development of authentic relationships rooted in a long-term commitment to social justice.

Our case study is drawn from a sociology course at Nottingham Trent University where there exists a distinguishing focus on public sociology – that is, a sociology that reaches beyond the university, creating opportunity for dialogue and change *with* the community, academics, students and diverse publics. The MA in Sociology, undertaken by about 18 students per year, includes a core service learning module extending across two terms. The module draws upon, reflects on and challenges the specific social, political and economic contexts of the city within which it's situated. Nottingham is the eighth most deprived city in England and is currently riven with issues from escalating child poverty to problems arising from rent arrears. The module looks not to rise above such issues but to engage actively and critically with them.

In the first term, MA students are introduced to core literature around service learning, drawing on the likes of Paolo Freire, Jane Adams and John Dewey. They critically reflect on service learning approaches, exploring tensions and complementarities between 'traditional' and 'critical' models. This work frames their second term where, as individuals, as pairs or in groups (the students decide), they source their own local community partners through which to undertake a service learning project. Students tend to choose partners based on their own prior lived or professional experiences and/or on issues that they're passionate about. Projects themselves are determined by the community partner and are usually small-scale pieces of research but can be more practical – for example, helping develop and run an event, designing volunteer recruitment processes and so on.

Crucially, service learning projects are rooted in the needs of the local community. The MA students negotiate a project brief with their chosen partner and complete a project form provided by the university that covers issues such as ethics procedures and risk assessments. The university also covers some expenses incurred by both students and communities and can provide additional help through the likes of providing rooms free of charge for associated meetings or events. Outside of this support, it's down to the MA students and community partners to keep projects on track.

Assessment is in two parts, both points occurring at the end of the second term. First, students create a poster that captures what they did during their project, notes any recommendations that arose and identifies any links to potential policy influence or impact. Posters need not be in a traditional academic style; students are encouraged to be creative in their presentation. The posters are displayed at an event to which community partners are invited, providing a fantastic platform to review and celebrate joint project work. This assessment point is worth 30%.

The remaining 70% is awarded through a 2,500-word reflective report where students draw critically on service learning literature to reflect on their service project and their experience of it. This includes exploring the extent to which their experiences fit the claims and ideals of critical service learning.

The module leader notes that the module always entails lots of emotional labour, not least because of the issues that are explored but also because of attendant tensions that frequently arise through limited resources, partnership working, time constraints and differences in organisational cultures. However, in uniting students and community partners around shared concerns, the resultant solidarity is often powerful enough to override such tensions. Nevertheless, it's best to start such modules small, doing them critically and well to demonstrate value and only scaling up when there are enough resources, both financial and human, to do so.

'Critical' service learning is underpinned by working with integrity; communities should never be conceived as a 'commodity' that students draw upon solely for their own personal or professional advantage. Mutuality is key. Whilst any single 'critical' service learning project can only achieve so much, their active coordination may help mobilise movements. In recognition of this, the Nottingham Trent team is looking to identify core local issues (e.g. rent arrears) around which students and community partners can rally to drive social change.

Whilst higher education institutions may continue to practice more 'traditional' approaches to social research that position the academy as 'in' but not 'of' society, 'critical' service learning provides an important rejoinder, a call to arms for research-informed activism.

5 Science shops

Related to

7 Business clinics
11 Consultancy and client-led briefs
3 'Traditional' and 4 'critical' service learning

In the field

Queen's University Belfast and Ulster University
University of Liverpool
University of Brighton

Typical assessment

Research report
Reflective practice
Presentation

Further reading

Beunen, R, Duineveld, M, During, R, Straver, G & Aalvanger, A (2012) Reflexivity in performative science shop projects. *Gateways: International Journal of Community Research and Engagement*, 5, pp 135–151

Zaal, R & Leydesdorff, L (1987) Amsterdam Science Shop and its influence on university research: The effects of ten years of dealing with non-academic questions. *Science and Public Policy*, 14(6), pp 310–316

See also

The Living Knowledge Network: www.livingknowledge.org

Summary

The science shop movement in Europe is by no means as ubiquitous as service learning (cross-reference Case Studies 3 and 4), but within the realms of 'real world' authentic learning, it's a crucial reference point and source of knowledge and practice. Developed in the 1960s and 1970s, science shops facilitate students working in partnership with local organisations on research problems that have been defined by the community. Science shops are a physical place (e.g. an office, website) and a person to whom communities can pose questions. For many external organisations, they act as a 'way in' to the university.

Science shops are unique amongst many of the examples in this book in that they're driven first and foremost by the research questions posed by civil society. Their ethos is to respond to community problems through research rather than to generate research questions. The starting point for any interaction with a science shop is a problem or question for which a civil society organisation is seeking research support. The questions that emerge are limitless in their possibility: from creating a map of toilets and benches for elderly and disabled members of the community, to conducting research on noise and air quality to inform objections to planning, through to business planning advice to small charities. They often incorporate multidisciplinary responses, combining social and human sciences, as well as natural, physical, engineering and technical sciences.

Science shops have been established to help bridge the structural, cultural and economic divide between science and civil society. They do this in three ways:

- providing access to 'research capacity' for non-governmental organisations and access to the community for students and researchers,
- through user-oriented techniques which emphasise participatory dialogue and methods,
- through providing research at little or no cost conducted by researchers and/or by students.

Now in its thirtieth year, the science shop at Queen's University Belfast and Ulster University is a joint endeavour supporting community organisations in developing research projects which are carried out by students as part of their degree programme. Over the past five years, the science shop has delivered 1,314 community research projects, with 4,894 students and 366 community organisations taking part. These groups have included sports clubs, youth groups and environmental organisations. Previous projects include urban design analysis of the West Belfast area in terms of thinking through good practice in planning for dementia, an investigation of the confidence and competency of crisis counsellors working with suicide and examining the experience of parenting a child with Down syndrome. Science shop staff work to identify appropriate resources and curriculum areas for the questions posed by communities, drawing on their rich knowledge of the university and its staff.

Science shops tend to focus their efforts on those that would otherwise not have access to scientific research. It's important that the research question not be commercially driven and that the results will be available in the public domain. An assessment is made of the client organisation's capacity to obtain the results/insights they need through other means, and all projects are assessed against ability to benefit the public good. Not all questions that are posed are immediately viable research projects. Science shops will develop the problem articulation with a client to set it at the right level. This translation role is central to the success of the science shop (for example, some questions will need to be expanded; others will need to be more tightly defined). The science shop is often resourced by a member of staff or team of staff who can act as an intermediary between the client and the university.

Science shop staff will also map the problem, once articulated, across the research expertise and capacity in the university, finding students and co-supervisors and building teams. Where science shop work is integrated into the curriculum, we typically see assessment of the end product (i.e. a client report or output). The assessment criteria will normally evaluate:

- methodological skills involved in assessing a client's needs and selecting appropriate research methods;
- analytical skills, including the development of theory;
- communication skills, for example, through a final report or presentation to the client;
- critical thinking about the context in which the research questions have been posed.

Some projects complement this with a reflective journal which is also assessed as part of the work. Science shop staff we spoke with stressed the importance of working with students beforehand to unpick their motivations to take on a project and work with specific communities.

Several interesting developments took place at the Queen's University Belfast and Ulster science shop, particularly around developing new spaces in the curriculum for this type of work. It's quite common to retrofit engagement onto existing curriculum, and what you tend to see here is the limitations of the traditional curriculum in two key ways: first in how a project is assessed – there's a division of focus between the external partner, who wants a report or output, and the academic tutor, who's looking to access the foundational knowledge. Combining these two pulls within one unit has been fruitful, but there's a lot more work to be done on this. The second development is how 'real world' problems can be used to drive interdisciplinarity. In many ways, the science shop facilitates interdisciplinary ways of working for the external partner. They often have students from multiple backgrounds working on discrete packages of work. However, there's a real potential to bring students together within one coherent programme.

6 Event management

Related to

8 Participatory arts
2 Public engagement
15 Placements

In the field (where to find examples)

Falmouth University
University of Surrey
University of Sunderland

Typical assessment

Portfolio
Reflective practice
Presentation

Further reading

Bossey, A (2019) Do graduating events management students perceive transformative benefits from experiential learning opportunities on a university's public events programme? *AEME Conference 2019: Festivals, Events and Well-Being Research*, University of Hertfordshire, 3 July
Bossey, A & Randell, J (2017) How can a professional box office system be utilised as a learning vehicle for events management students? *AEME Conference: Event Futures: Innovation, Creativity and Collaboration*, Cardiff Metropolitan University, 4 July
Ryan, W R (2016) How do you 'do' event management education? A case study of event management higher education awards. *Event Management*, 20, pp 69–80

Summary

Event management is a field of study in its own right, having emerged originally from drama and hospitality provision in the United Kingdom and United States, and is now a popular degree option at over 70 British universities. It's also a delivery technique that can be deployed in virtually any degree programme. Subjects as diverse as chemistry, sport and English literature incorporate event management modules or units, and the approach is valued for its ability to foster collaboration, imagination and understanding. At the level of a module, the basic proposition is for students to work collectively in order to deliver an event which communicates subject knowledge or inspires discussion, connects directly with the relevant professional realm or works with a community or market of importance to the course or institution.

Our example is drawn from the provision at Falmouth University, where the successful creative events management degree incorporates the delivery of live events in a way that could be transferable to other subjects but which also relies on partnerships within and beyond the host institution. Falmouth's particular geographic and strategic position means that events can be targeted at a wide range of markets, from students at the two universities that are now such a feature of the town, to local community groups, to corporates and small and medium-sized enterprises in the regional economy and beyond. The university hosts a public-facing Academy of Music and Theatre Arts, with studios designed for small-scale performances, and has other campus spaces that can be utilised for a variety of occasions.

Students work within the curriculum to deliver three live events, which are staged through dedicated modules across the three years of the degree. The logistical and intellectual challenge increases as the course progresses. In their first year, students select from a menu of events, all of which are delivered in the Academy of Music and Theatre Arts. Staff provide significant scaffolding in terms of risk assessment and oversight at this stage. As they progress, students take greater ownership of the core idea and gradually move the location of their event beyond the campus to work with external partners. The challenge of the third year extends the students' sense of agency and responsibility and forces them to work in multiagency partnerships, complicating the analysis required for successful negotiations and the management problems faced in delivery. In all cases, the events are authentic in the sense that members of various local communities register, attend and offer feedback voluntarily. If students encounter challenges or failures – if, for example, they are unable to secure or engage an audience – this learning can be accounted for through reflections and other aspects of their assessment.

Given the nature of the institution, the focus of the Falmouth projects tends to be on arts and culture, but many students extend their gaze to other realms and sectors, including tourism, business development, higher education outreach and sustainability. In most cases, students work in project teams of four and collaborate in order to conceive, plan, deliver and review an event. The core knowledge relates to project management and also to effective planning and logistics, including budgeting, marketing and evaluation. The core skills relate to learning, communication, negotiation and team working. Knowledge is assessed through written proposals and plans, which include the production of an 'event pack' made available for assessment at the delivery stage. The pack is designed to cover all of the key logistical elements, including the approach to risk assessment. Skills are assessed through a mixture of presentations (including an early-stage 'pitch to industry' in the final year module), assessment of event delivery and reflective practice assignments. The reflective element is present in the modules at each level.

In the Falmouth case, the students are encouraged to reflect on the ways in which they respond to team dynamics, interactions with partner agencies and critical incidents. All assessment is individual; no marks are awarded directly for performance in the group, although practice varies across institutions on this count.

A wide range of partner agencies now support the events, and trust in the process has been built over time. Alumni of the course are now events managers or sponsors in their own right and continue to contribute to the community of learning as hosts, mentors or members of employer-pitch panels. Although the development of this network has taken considerable time and energy, its value is now considerable and offers students significant opportunities within and beyond their studies. Feedback from external stakeholders is consistently positive, and students attest to the impact of the live events on their learning and employability. Overall satisfaction is high.

In transferring the live event mode to another discipline or field of study, considerations should include the complexity and location of the event and the extent to which staff provide scaffolding, including guidance on risk assessments and management. Although reflective practice is the dominant mode of assessment for this approach, evaluations of impact on the audience or the partners could be considered, as could more detailed consideration of the team performance and interactions. Peer assessment, in various forms, could therefore be deployed, and it could also be possible to draw external partners more directly into the assessment realm.

7 Business clinics

Related to

1 Legal clinics
11 Consultancy and client-led briefs
9 Trading entities

In the field

Northumbria University

Typical assessment

Group presentation
Reflective practice
Final year report

Further reading

Coates, N & Wijayaratna, K (2015) NBS UG consultancy project. In *The Compendium of Effective Practices in Direct Independent Learning*. York: QAA & the Higher Education Academy

National Centre for Universities and Business (2019) *State of the Relationship Report*. London: NCUB

See also

Final Report & How To Guide (2019): Digitally Enabled Business Clinic – a cost-effective means of universities supporting SMEs to increase their productivity, project number: 22526, Competition: Business Basics: boosting SME productivity (proof of concept strand), https://drive.google.com/drive/folders/1 XomlkaVUj9UzRnr5iP4F1cB3JLRRjeFP?usp=sharing

Summary

The Business Clinic at Northumbria University is, as far as we can tell, the only example of its kind in the United Kingdom. Building on the success of an earlier legal clinic at the institution, it started life in 2013 and has grown to the point where it occupies its own purpose-built facility complete with meeting spaces, boardroom and Harvard lecture–style theatre, offering services to over 100 client organisations and supporting some 400 students each academic year.

The clinic houses the activities of final-year undergraduate and MA students on business-related courses, including marketing, finance, human resources and accountancy. Working in groups of four, the students address a challenge or problem brought to them by a local business or charitable organisation. On the basis of desk research, teamwork and expert supervision by academic staff, the groups produce a consultancy report that guides the client organisation towards solutions. The service is provided pro bono, and the client list now includes small and medium-sized enterprises from the locality, as well as a number of well-known multinationals and not-for-profits. Dedicated academic staff at the clinic work with clients to refine project briefs, allocate topics to groups and then support each team as they develop solutions.

For undergraduate students, the experience with the Business Clinic represents their final year or 'capstone' project, enabling them to build on and synthesize knowledge gleaned during the rest of their degree. The module is therefore an alternative to the traditional dissertation, and while it still has a research component, the emphasis is more applied and more collaborative, arguably reflecting the increasing employer requirements for transferable skills. Students are assessed using a combination of group reports and presentations, linked directly to the nature of the consultation, and then a literature review and reflection, which anchors the project in academic literature.

The module extends across two semesters and is worth 40 credits. It begins with a preparatory phase where students form their own groups and then complete a series of team-building exercises, gradually developing their understanding of their own skills and strengths. Each team is allocated two supervisors in this period. During this time, staff members also work with clients, refining their projects and agreeing on the briefs that will be ultimately communicated to students. This work with the clients is regarded as crucial to quality control for all parties, ensuring that the level and amount of work are sufficiently ambitious and achievable. Specific projects are then allocated by staff to the student groups, ensuring that effective matching takes place, accounting for the skills mix in particular teams. Exploratory meetings between the student groups and the client organisation then take place at the Clinic site, and the project begins.

Students continue their group work in studio settings at the clinic, meeting for two hours per week, working with their supervisor and committing to further engagement with the client where required. Visits to client premises often help to enhance relationships and improve the end-product but are not compulsory. Projects address a diverse range of organisational challenges, including product and workforce development, recruitment, diversification, inclusion, marketing and change management. They may require the student groups to engage in primary research or the generation of ideas and solutions on the basis of current research or reviews of best practice. The final product is delivered to the client in two elements, a group presentation and a jointly authored consultancy report. The learning and development of each individual student is then captured in the literature review and reflective essay.

External partners are consistently positive about the experience and value both the interaction with students and the guidance that emerges at the end of the process. Increasingly, students are working on projects of considerable significance to the clients, which in turn has required staff to develop non-disclosure agreements and to manage these on behalf of the university. Staff at the clinic therefore require subject and supervisory expertise but also the ability to manage risk on behalf of all parties and to negotiate confidentiality and consent. This time spent explaining terms and conditions is considered of great value and provides effective scaffolding for the learning of both the students and the external clients.

The process for students at the masters level is essentially the same – they work in groups of four and are supported in a similar manner. However, the level and nature of the challenge will shift, and projects will be allocated appropriately. Students at all levels report very positive experiences, with many building associations with client organisations that lead to extended networks and even job opportunities in some instances.

Since 2013, the Northumbria Business Clinic has supported over 300 businesses, worked with over 1,200 students and delivered consultancy to the estimated value of £1.6 million. Its position at the concluding stage of the degree is a point of difference with legal clinics, which tend to be optional and between second and third years. Like legal clinics, though, business clinics have the potential to link to other areas of university business, enabling some cross-selling and growth around knowledge transfer and exchange. The Northumbria example centres on knowledge from business-related fields, but it's conceivable that many other disciplines or fields could be deployed in a similar fashion.

8 Participatory arts

Related to

10 Applied theatre
4 'Critical' service learning
18 Design agency

In the field

University of South Wales
University of Brighton
University of the Highlands and Islands

Typical assessment

Idea pitches
Artwork
Explanatory text

Further reading

Pickard, B (2019) The process, challenges and opportunities of developing a curriculum in a creative and therapeutic arts undergraduate degree programme. *International Journal of Art and Design Education*. doi:10.1111/jade.12226
Schlemmer, R H (2017) Socially engaged art education: Defining and defending the practice. In L N Hersey & B Bobick (eds) *Handbook of Research on the Facilitation of Civic Engagement Through Community Art*. Hershey, PA: IGI Global. pp 1–20

See also
ArtWorks Cymru (2015) *Quality Principles*. Available at: https://artworks.cymru/quality-principles

Summary

Participatory arts pedagogies draw on critical, educational and artistic practices designed to forge interactions between artists and communities focused on social issues (Schlemmer, 2017). Risk-taking and rule-breaking are considered positive attributes within art and design education, with uncertainty valued, as it prompts critical, creative and lateral thinking skills.

ArtWorks Cymru (2015) suggest that quality principles for participatory arts programmes – ways of thinking about, valuing and enhancing participatory arts practices – can be grouped under three areas:

1   *Intention* – catalysing social change through being artistic and professional; relevant and inclusive and inspiring, challenging and engaging;

2   *People* – practices that are participant centred, focused on participant transformation through shared ownership and responsibility;
3   *Activity* – activities that are collaboratively planned, suitably situated and resourced, active, hands-on and reflective.

Our case study comes from the BA (Hons) Creative & Therapeutic Arts degree at the University of South Wales, wherein second-year students undertake an Open Call project as part of an art module. Students are tasked with producing original artwork over the course of one semester for the corridors of St Woolos Hospital. Over several years, the project has been delivered in partnership with an arts-in-health charity, Gwent Arts in Health (Garth), based in St Woolos.

Each year, Garth produces a brief for the students. The 2019 brief was to design a series of framed photographs or digital prints to enhance the public spaces of St Woolos, to celebrate the positive impact the NHS has on individuals and society and to consider what healthcare may look like in the future. Garth was particularly interested in interpretations of real-life NHS stories from staff and retirees in the local area and beyond.

Throughout the Open Call project, various engagement points between Garth, St Woolos and the students occur. Around two weeks after release of the artist brief, a site visit and engagement session are arranged for students to meet members of the NHS community and to capture real-life voices and stories through arts-based methods in order to inform artworks. Midway through the semester, Garth gives feedback on works in progress, suggesting ways they could be developed and ensuring appropriateness for the audience. The course concludes with an exhibition event, celebrating the artworks in situ, and to which participants, staff, family and friends are invited. At this event, students typically make an introductory speech about their artwork, run a creative evaluation event and read out poems or special texts that they've created for the day.

For the 2019 iteration of the project, a public arts commissioner – Studio Response – was involved alongside Garth, as they were sourcing works for a new hospital in Llanfrechfa and thought the project could be a way for students to win fee-paying commissions. Studio Response have provided both support (e.g. critical feedback to students) and funding (e.g. for printing and framing of the artworks) in return for involvement with the project.

Ninety percent of course assessment is based on the artwork produced, specifically:

- The refinement of presentation (framing, mounting, curation etc.)
- The clarity of concept (how the viewer interacts with the piece)
- The artistic skills
- The appropriateness to the arts and health context (providing educational learning for the viewer, opportunities for meditation etc.)
- The extent of creativity in response to the brief

The remaining 10% is awarded for explanatory text, which must be no more than 100 words and must add richness to the viewer experience and acknowledge participants' voices.

In engaging with communities and institutions, students face contexts that may constrain their artworks and/or shape their voice. For example, within a hospital setting, artworks must be reproducible (i.e. possessing no great financial value) and wipeable, for hygiene reasons. Great sensitivity to audience – an awareness of the therapeutic context – is essential, as patients may revisit artworks multiple times, using them as prompts for reflection or as conversation starters. Students who have previously imagined themselves as activists, as risk-takers and rule-breakers, may come to recognise that with power comes responsibility and that their works must be attuned to ethics and politics within institutional contexts. This can prove frustrating for some.

Despite the potential for such frustration, students appreciate the fact that their work is displayed publicly and is recognised by professional organisations. Indeed, many say the project demystifies the professional world and develops their sense of pride via production of a commissioned piece. Garth has noted that its involvement has helped raise its profile and networks across St Woolos. Hospital staff who see themselves in the artworks feel better understood, and the artworks themselves have been used as reference points for occupational health specialists challenging patients to walk as far as a particular piece.

The course convenor recognises how long it takes to design and deliver the Open Call project – sourcing money and briefs, maintaining communication with external partners and supporting students all takes time. Public display of the artworks adds a layer of risk. Some past pieces have been political and critical of the NHS, so Garth now reviews works in progress to ensure that any controversial ideas are presented in ways appropriate for context, whilst explanatory texts state that all views are those of the artists alone.

Despite such challenges, the value of the participatory arts approach remains in enabling students to work alongside professionals, to critically reflect on institutional contexts and to unleash the potential of creative practices to enhance wellbeing.

9 Trading entities

Related to

7 Business clinics
19 Vertically integrated projects
18 Design agency

In the field

Bishop Grosseteste University
Falmouth University
University of the West of England

Typical assessment

Business, marketing and budgeting plans
Pitches and presentations
Reflective practice

Further reading

Hyams-Ssekasi, D & Caldwell, E (eds) (2018) *Experiential Learning for Entrepreneurship: Theoretical and Practical Perspectives on Enterprise Education.* London: Palgrave Macmillan

Tosey, P, Dhaliwal, S & Hassinen, J (2013) The Finnish Team Academy model: Implications for management education. *Management Learning*, 46, pp 175–194

Summary

Trading entities are a response to the challenge of how to engage students in the bodies of knowledge that relate to business and enterprise. Without direct experience, the fundamentals of finance, marketing, logistics and human resource management can be received as abstract and 'dry' and force students into superficial engagement with learning pathways and materials. Work-based learning, in the form of short-term or sandwich placements, is one answer to this problem but is constrained in the sense that students are nearly always subordinate in these settings. While it's understandable that placement students should experience organisations from a particular perspective and that a trainee position makes practical sense in this context, these factors tend towards an experience where a student cannot make decisions, stretch their imagination or utilise their considerable agency.

This is of particular note where the intended outcome of an education is to facilitate leadership or enterprising behaviour. There's an expectation that managers and entrepreneurs will necessarily learn by doing; will take risks and get things wrong and will regard making mistakes as simply another step on their learning journey. The importance of these aspects of learning has led colleagues at a range of institutions to find ways of providing actual businesses that provide students with the opportunities to run organisations, to make decisions, to trade and to manage the consequences of these actions. In some cases, these organisations are owned by the institutions, in others by individual students, in others by collectives or partnerships. In all of them, students are given ownership and the ability to determine their own fate.

Trading entities can be experienced horizontally or vertically through a degree (in the course of a single year or across an entire programme) and can represent a part or whole of the student experience. They can trade with markets on campus or beyond the campus and are restricted only by the objectives in the entity's constitution. They may be social enterprises, limited companies or ring-fenced 'entities' within the university itself.

The BA Business (Team Entrepreneurship) at Bishop Grosseteste University provides our case study for this approach. Here, each cohort of students is supported to set up and run a business entity for the three years of their degree. Under the umbrella of the business, teams of students pursue projects and endeavours that shape and develop their approaches to leadership and enterprise. The entity is dissolved at the end of the degree, but individuals are then free to pursue the ideas that they have originated as part of their studies.

Students learn through the business in two distinct ways. First, they engage in 'learning labs' where they develop their business ideas and applications with the support of a qualified team coach – an academic member of staff. Second, they explore the theoretical underpinnings of their ideas through action learning sets. This strand facilitates critical enquiry and reflection. Students are encouraged to follow their ideas from conception through to execution and to apply theoretical constructs to each stage of their journey. Success, failure, conflict, competition and co-operation are all possible outcomes for the enterprise activities, but the assessment regime for the course ensures that students can progress on the basis of what they have gleaned from their adventures. Assessment tasks include those that engage with underpinning knowledge – literature reviews, market research, the development of academic resources – those that engage with specific enterprise skills – presenting, pitching, planning – and those that support reflective practice.

The Bishop Grosseteste course is also founded on the Team Academy philosophy, an educational approach developed in the 1990s in Finland, which emphasises choice, responsibility and creativity. The 'no lectures, no exams' character of the course is derived from these principles, as is the central role of the team coach, whose expertise in facilitation helps the students to understand and develop their collaborative skills and to manage the balance between freedom, responsibility and action. In the Finnish context, graduates are already taking ideas from their educative experience and turning them into viable, self-sustaining businesses. The same outcome is anticipated at Bishop Grosseteste, with the caveat that the business that students shared throughout the duration of the course has to be dissolved on graduation. Any remaining surplus is divided up between the participating students.

This collective approach differs in character to those where the focus is on the individual entrepreneur. In these settings, individual students will receive 'incubation' support from universities and their various business partners, often in 'growth hub' or 'innovation' centres. The journey into enterprise provides the student with authentic experience, and this is captured by an assessment regime. Typically, this mode is utilised in the postgraduate realm.

Other potential approaches could involve an entity which rolls on from year to year and which is reformed and refreshed by the students who own or lead it for the period in question or one in which the incubation services are offered to individuals at a later stage of development, perhaps after graduation.

10 Applied theatre

Related to

8 Participatory arts
4 'Critical' service learning
18 Design agency

In the field

Goldsmiths, University of London
Birmingham City University
Royal Central School of Speech & Drama

Typical assessment

Reflective portfolio
Workshop project
Presentation

Further reading

Danvers, J (2003) Towards a radical pedagogy: Provisional notes on learning and teaching in art and design. *International Journal of Art & Design Education*, 22(1), pp 47–57
Hunter, M (2008) Cultivating the art of safe space. *Research in Drama Education: The Journal of Applied Theatre and Performance*, 13(1), pp 5–21
Preston, S (2016) *Applied Theatre: Facilitation – Pedagogies, Practices, Resilience.* London: Bloomsbury

Summary

Applied theatre is an established term that's widely associated with creative practices that engage with the social, educational and political functions of theatrical processes (Hughes and Nicholson, 2016). It's often underpinned by activist rhetoric, concerned with both personal and social change. As such, pedagogic goals of 'learning to be' are valued over 'learning about', whilst 'learning by doing' is an essential component.

As with other participatory arts pedagogies, applied theatre appreciates critical, lateral thinking and creative skills, encouraging students to develop new ways of looking at existing problems and identifying new opportunities for creative practices. It trades on a "pedagogy of ambiguity" (Danvers, 2003); that is, it's an educational philosophy grounded in constructivism, underpinned by a belief that learning is based on divergent rather than convergent thinking and entails some change in one's values, beliefs, ideas or ways of being, knowing and doing. Collaboration to enhance political engagement and cultural awareness is core to applied theatre pedagogy.

Our case study comes from the MA in Applied Theatre: Drama in Educational, Community & Social Contexts at Goldsmiths, a degree that recruits people from backgrounds in theatre, education, activism or social change. The module in question – The Reflexive Practitioner – is optional, delivered via ten three-hour-long workshops over the course of a semester. It was conceived in 2012 by Goldsmiths and two other organisations – Emergency Exit Arts, an outdoor arts company, and Talawa, the United Kingdom's primary Black-led touring theatre company. Through the module, students have the opportunity to design and deliver an applied theatre workshop for a designated audience to gain a greater understanding of the art and craft of both facilitation and collaboration. Through their practice, they must reflect and act on their reflections whilst challenging their assumptions.

Around 15 MA students study the module each year, which, uniquely, they undertake in collaboration with five students from Talawa's Creating Routes programme. That programme is open to theatre-makers aged between 18 and 25 years old and from Black and minority ethnic backgrounds, providing them with opportunities to develop the knowledge, skills and experience needed to gain employment in the participatory arts sector.

Through the module, MA and Creating Routes students are divided into four groups and collaborate to develop their workshop. Groups are assigned a particular target audience. In the past, audiences have included primary and secondary school children; young people not in education, employment or training and social work undergraduate students. Each group decides on the particular theme for its applied theatre workshop, one best suited to the target audience.

In terms of course structure, following an introductory session to the module, groups undertake four three-hour-long sessions to design their workshops, the final session of which involves feedback on their plans. The subsequent four sessions see each of the groups take it in turn to facilitate its workshop with its set audiences, whilst the remaining groups either observe or participate. Thus, all groups have the experience of co-facilitation, observation and participation. The final session of the course focuses on reflection and evaluation, where groups are encouraged to name their learning.

For the MA students, there's one assessment point – a 3,000-word, reflective, mixed-media portfolio. Crucially, the assessment isn't of the workshop itself but rather of the individual student's level of reflection about it and their role within it. Students must articulate learning that took place through their practice, their situated learning about drama facilitation and the ethics of collaboration. The course convenor notes that commonly, students struggle with at least one of their roles as observer, co-facilitator or participant, experiencing discomfort that can provide a rich basis for reflection.

There's no formal assessment for the Creating Routes students, but their involvement in the module helps them to better understand what it is that they wish to do professionally. In addition, they attend six Saturday sessions outside of the module that cover core issues and ideas behind the participatory arts (e.g. safeguarding, power and privilege, diversity and inclusion etc.).

Given the origins and nature of the module, it's rooted in mutual benefit, time and goodwill of all organisations involved; no financial contributions are made. For Goldsmiths, the close connection with practitioners is key, providing students with applied learning opportunities and enabling both practice-informed research and research-informed practice.

Tensions can and do arise. The reality of participatory arts is that work takes place with communities where structures are lacking, where last-minute cancellations or a lack of communication can arise. This can be stressful for students who are working within structured university semesters and to set timescales.

The course convenor also notes challenges within groups arising from stereotypes that the MA and Creating Routes students initially have of one another. Broadly, the former can stereotype the latter as of the 'real world', full of artistic confidence, whilst the latter can perceive the former as 'academic' and 'clever' but divorced from the 'real world.' Grains of truth may exist in these stereotypes; they speak to complicated issues of identity and power dynamics that exist between and within the different sets of students. In order to establish productive collaborations oriented towards shared goals, students are encouraged to reflect on these issues, noting the likes of when they do and don't feel comfortable, who's speaking and who's silent in certain situations and so on.

In sum, this case demonstrates the value of partnership working between universities and community arts organisations, work that is never about 'serving' or 'gifting' the community but rather about mutuality.

11 Consultancy projects and client-led briefs

Related to

7 Business clinics
14 Live projects
3 'Traditional' service learning

In the field

University of Bristol
University College London
University of East Anglia

Typical assessment

Report for client
Reflective practice
Presentation

Further reading

O'Hara, S, Reeve, S & Flowers, S (2003) The live consultancy case study. In R Kemp & D Hawkridge (eds) *Learning and Teaching for Business*. London: Kogan Page
Owen, D & Hill, S (2011) *Embedding Public Engagement in the Curriculum: A Framework for the Assessment of Student Learning from Public Engagement*. Bristol: National Co-Ordinating Centre for Public Engagement

See also

A toolkit on design thinking for educators at: https://designthinkingforeduca-tors.com

Summary

Consultancy projects and client-led briefs provide a way in which the skills and knowledge students have in many different disciplines can be offered to external communities. It's a popular approach used in IT, business and management, engineering, architecture and wide range of social sciences. It can also be used at different curriculum levels.

Students can work individually, but often, particularly at the undergraduate level, students will work in mixed teams of up to three to five students undertaking a bespoke research project to address problems and challenges set by external organisations. The range of different client groups that this approach is accessible to is one part of the appeal. At the University of Bristol, for example, the Centre for Innovation and Entrepreneurship has been setting up client-led briefs with partners as diverse as a telecommunication company looking at future technology, through to a local MP looking to find new ways to engage constituents. Projects cover a range of motives, from those more socially engaged such as improving employability outcomes for young people with autism or those that aim to influence policy, to projects with more commercially driven outcomes. Organisations in different sectors might gain new insights about a challenge their organisation is facing and a deeper understanding of their end user. They may also gain inspiration through the literature review and other secondary research conducted to inform the project.

Across UK higher education institutions (HEIs), consultancy projects offer external organisations a wide range of opportunities, including, for example:

- Literature reviews to support the writing of policy documents and publications
- Supply chain analysis
- Market research
- Compilation of databases and directories
- Production of workshop materials
- Support with the development of communications campaigns
- Support with event management and stakeholder engagement
- Systems analysis
- Information management
- Web design
- Feasibility studies

As with other forms of authentic learning, time is required to support the development of projects with partners, ensuring that projects are theoretically rich and that students are able to meet expectations. Most of the projects we encountered took place within 8–12-week timescales. This enabled enough time for students to come to terms with the brief, lay the necessary foundations, conduct field work and prepare a report or presentation to the client.

Consulting methods can be used to facilitate vertical integration between cohorts. At Bristol's Centre for Innovation and Entrepreneurship, we found scaffolded experiences for different year groups within a programme. For example, students in the first year work on a slightly more hypothetical, lower-risk project, while the second- or third-years work in a more hands-on way with a real client. Throughout their programme, they try to diversify the types of projects, so students get experience working with different partners and across different sectors. This approach has been adopted by the university to embed innovation across all disciplines with the availability of a four-year integrated master's programme. Students in this programme are supported through their experiential learning with modules on systems and design thinking.

The University of Bristol's MSc in environmental and policy management also utilises consultancy projects as a central part of its approach to teaching and learning. The approach is a key aspect of its marketing, and students have worked with a wide range of partners in the past, including government bodies (e.g. Defra, Ministry of Defence, Bristol City Council), private sector firms (e.g. Arup, Burgess Salmon, Resource Futures, Triodos Bank), nongovernmental organisations (NGOs; e.g. International Emissions Trading Association, Sustrans, WRAP) and multilateral agencies (e.g. International Energy Agency). The programme aims to give students a practical yet critical grounding in environmental consultancy and management, developing skills that will help students become effective. Unit aims include the skills and techniques needed for problem framing and analysis, research project management, communications and reflective skills. Whilst learning is highly experiential, students are guided through the consultancy projects with a range of seminars and facilitated sessions guided by an academic mentor. Seminars and facilitated sessions cover a range of areas, such as:

- Organising and forming a team
- Client communication: defining a brief, diagnosis and discovery, managing relationships, reporting
- Problem definition and analysing
- Participation skills
- Stakeholder mapping
- Project management and finances
- Ethics and health and safety

Significant in this example was that client feedback contributes to 10% of the overall mark of the consultancy module.

Other notable examples of the consultancy approach include Interchange at the University of Liverpool. Here the focus is solely on voluntary and community organisations (VCOs), and its helps the organisation interpret a specific piece of legislation/social policy or address a knowledge gap within the organisation. Another interesting example is the evaluation exchange at University College London. Framed predominantly as an opportunity for postgraduate students, it provides much-needed evaluation consultancy services to VCOs. Students form a collaborative partnership with a VCO in East London to tackle an evaluation challenge (such as designing an evaluation plan, developing surveys, analysing existing data). Through this programme, students can help embed the use of successful evaluation approaches.

Academics we spoke with felt that consultancy projects presented distinct opportunities for students. Advantages included their time-bound nature and that students were often tasked with 'nice-to-have' but desirable projects for partners, focused on learning and discovery, rather than delivering core business. It was also noted that the process of working with external partners to clarify a brief was a crucial learning opportunity. In some cases, academics raised concerns that consultancy projects did not always provide a theoretically challenging problem for students. Without effective module design, ensuring that engagement was embedded in the learning outcomes, this could present problems as students find themselves split between providing two outputs: a report for the client which advances *the client's* understanding of an issue and a report for a tutor which draws on a sound theoretical base and advances *the knowledge* base surrounding that issue. Nevertheless, we heard many examples of where these two aspects of theory and application had been usefully combined. A final risk that people noted was the level of variability in consultancy projects; as with so many forms of authentic learning, there is much that happens in the real world that tutors cannot control.

12 Field courses

Related to

15 Placements
19 Vertically integrated projects
13 Living labs

In the field (where to find examples)

University of Gloucestershire
University of Chester
University of Reading

Typical assessment

Field notes
Project report
Reflective practice

Further reading

Goodenough, A, Derounian, J, Lynch, K, Hart, A, Roberts, H, Evans, M & Hurley, W (2015) *For Real: Forming Resilience and Employability Through Authentic Learning, 2015 Action Research Report*. York: Higher Education Academy.

Goodenough, A, Rolfe, R, MacTavish, L & Hart, A (2015) The role of overseas field courses in student learning in the biosciences. *Bioscience Education*. doi:10.11120/beej.2014.00021

Hart, A, Stafford, R & Goodenough, A (2011) Bridging the lecturer/student divide: The role of residential field courses. *Bioscience Education*, 17(1), pp 1–5

Summary

Fieldwork has a long history and is intimately entwined with the development of higher knowledge in a wide range of disciplines, from anthropology to biology to geography. It describes the research activity of collecting data on environments, species and habitats or human communities in situ. Fieldwork can take several forms, including short sessions, day fieldtrips and residential field courses; the last of these is the focus of this case study.

A field course is a period of learning that takes place away from campus-based classrooms or laboratories at a site of relevance to the discipline or topic of study. This can serve a number of purposes, and these vary by subject specialism and by the level of learning. Field courses can be utilised in order to enable students to link theory and practice, to engage directly with research skills, to create situations that facilitate immersion with the subject or context or to build community and connections. In some cases, field courses are used explicitly in order to break down barriers between staff and students, to provide opportunities for all members of a subject community to work shoulder to shoulder and to recognise the strengths and skills that all contributors may bring to an endeavour.

Field courses can be deployed in the extracurricular realm, but they frequently carry credit, either as an aspect of a module or as a whole unit of learning. They can be for any unit of time, from a portion of a day to a month or more. Longer options are often residential and therefore afford an opportunity for informality that's not present in the controlled environment of traditional learning. The combination of additional responsibility and independence, active learning, community building and problem solving that often characterise extended field courses mean that they're often presented as sites where transformational learning can take place. Students engage more deeply in their subject in these settings and reflect on their capacities as a learner as well as a potential employee. The challenges that they face in unfamiliar environments often stimulate a new approach to their studies and their discipline while simultaneously building identity and resilience.

Our example of field courses comes from the University of Gloucestershire, an institution with a long history of immersive techniques and active learning. The School of Natural and Social Sciences has, for almost a decade, run annual residential field courses to enable undergraduate and postgraduates to undertake fieldwork in a novel location – Mankwe Wildlife Reserve in South Africa. The course lasts for two weeks and is offered as an optional module for second-year students in BSc biology and also as a project module for MSc students in related programmes. Typically, two or three members of staff accompany 30 students for the two-week course in Mankwe – mostly undergraduates but up to a third postgraduate. Both groups are given preparatory training experiences and tasks to complete in advance of the trip; this includes project design work for the postgraduates who pursue independent research projects while at the reserve.

The experiences of the students are shaped in order to reflect the needs of the staff at the reserve. Students will normally engage with a range of ecological survey skills, collecting important monitoring data on mammals (including zebra, giraffe and many different antelope species), birds, invertebrates and vegetation. They'll also consider and engage with a range of contemporary challenges facing the reserve through the completion of a negotiated group project. The work of the undergraduates is more obviously structured than the experiences of the postgraduates, whose projects are negotiated in advance with the reserve and who proceed with greater independence and responsibility. In both cases, data of benefit to all parties are generated. Project work has led to a series of staff and student co-publications, including outputs that have incorporated the work of staff at the reserve.

A range of assessment devices is deployed in order to structure and capture learning. While the postgraduates face exercises that reflect the process of research production – notably the preparation of an individual 5,000-word project report and a viva examination – the undergraduates submit a field-work notebook (including notes, details of survey protocols, field sketches, line maps, diagrams, data and reflections on findings) and submit a short individual write-up of their group project – these together equate to 3,000 words. Support for all assessment formats is offered before, during and after the trip itself.

The long-term nature of the relationship between Gloucestershire and Mankwe means that staff and students can build on the knowledge and experience of their peers and can participate in the generation of long-term temporal data that has utility for the reserve and for scientific communities more widely. This mutuality is evidenced most obviously in the wide range of publications that have emanated from the course, from discipline-specific outputs to pedagogical papers and presentations. It also creates an environment for students to experience challenge and transformation, in which they feel that their contribution is both genuine and valued by all stakeholders.

Field courses clearly have many benefits, but they also require different kinds of skills from academic staff, who need to be prepared for the vagaries of travel and group formation and be capable of supporting students in new and challenging circumstances. Institutions require appropriate expertise in risk assessment, insurance, budgeting and travel, and should be prepared to facilitate curricular activity out of term time. The students, meanwhile, need to be willing to challenge themselves and to work with others, but unfortunately, in most cases, they need to pay. The cost of international field courses tends to fall on the participants and is additional to course fees, so issues of access and privilege may be one barrier that colleagues have to traverse carefully in future.

13 Living labs

Related to

14 Live projects
22 Student action
12 Field courses

In the field

University of Leicester
University of Edinburgh
University of Leeds

Typical assessment

Dissertations
Presentations
Project reports

Further reading

Favaloro, T, Ball, T & Lipschutz, R D (2019) Mind the gap! Developing the campus as a living lab for student experiential learning in sustainability. In W Leal Filho & U Bardi (eds) *Sustainability on University Campuses: Learning, Skills Building and Best Practices. World Sustainability Series.* Springer: Cham. pp 91–113
Safitri Zen, I, D'Souza, C, Ishmail, S & Arsat, M (2019) University living learning labs: An integrative and transformative approach. *Journal of Sustainability Science and Management*, 14(4), pp 139–155

See also

For practical tips and resources about living labs, see the Environmental Association for Universities and Colleges (EUAC) website here: www.eauc. org.uk/eauc_living_labs_project

Summary

Living labs – a pedagogic concept rather than a physical space – can be applied to contexts both within and beyond campus boundaries. Whatever the setting, the pedagogy emphasises projects that provide hands-on experiences for students, the opportunity for them to apply their skills and classroom theory to 'real world' problems. A pedagogy supporting experiential learning, living lab projects act as platforms for creative ideas, encouraging open innovation approaches that optimise the work capabilities of stakeholders involved (Safitri Zen et al., 2019).

Living lab projects explore any and all societal issues, but within the United Kingdom and elsewhere, they're most commonly used to confront the challenges of becoming sustainable, challenges faced by university campuses themselves. As such, living labs present ideal encounters for students to focus on sustainability, utilising multidisciplinary perspectives to engage with complex issues and to suggest how wicked issues might be tackled in ways that enhance sustainability (Favaloro et al., 2019).

The University of Leicester has implemented just such an approach, coordinated by the University's Social Impact Team based in Estates & Campus Services. That team launched a living lab approach several years ago as a means to generate collaborative undergraduate or postgraduate research projects – those bringing together students, academic staff, professional services staff and/or external actors – to explore real-life sustainability problems related to any of the United Nations' 17 Sustainable Development Goals (SDGs). Focus on the SDGs allows for research projects that stretch beyond simple environmental conceptions of sustainability to encompass social issues such as poverty and inequality. In so doing, the living lab fosters inter- and multidisciplinary perspectives.

At any given time, the Social Impact Team has a list of current projects that students could research, but students may also develop their own research projects in conversation with the team; around seven projects are undertaken each year. Alongside conducting a rigorous piece of academic research to address the issue at hand, students produce a one-page summary of their findings which they may present to relevant working groups or teams. This encourages them to elicit the 'so what?' of their research project, highlighting its implications for a professional, not just academic, audience. Students are particularly motivated by the notion that their research might make a difference, might mobilise change; the focus on sustainability taps into the activist tendencies of many. Two of Leicester's students won national Green Gown awards for the impact of their projects.

In the last couple of years, the Social Impact Team has looked beyond research projects, building the living lab approach into taught modules in order to reach greater numbers of students. For example, in a Research Methods in Marketing module for an MSc (Hons) in marketing, teams of students are presented with the same project brief, a sustainability-related challenge – for example, to tackle the issue of coffee cup disposal on campus – and tasked with designing solutions. Thus, multiple ideas and solutions are crowdsourced for the same issue. Teams produce reports based on their solutions and pitch them initially to their tutor group and then to the university's Social Impact Team, who pick a winner. There's then the very real chance that the winning group's ideas will be implemented. Around 100 students partake in this module each year.

Teams across Estates & Campus Services – from social impact to carbon and energy, gardens to waste – are core to providing ideas and data for living lab projects, and those students undertaking research projects always meet with the relevant Estates team to discuss further. The Estates teams benefit from the relatively rare opportunity (for them) of engaging with students, who provide a fresh pair of eyes on problems that might otherwise appear intractable. And the students are often better attuned to the needs and perspectives of their peers, enhancing the likely efficacy or traction of proposed solutions. Finally, alongside transcending disciplinary silos, the living lab approach also crosses boundaries between professional services and academic staff, fostering dialogue between the two, and beyond building maintenance issues!

As the living lab is coordinated by a professional services team at Leicester, it can be difficult to secure meetings with academics, who may initially wonder about the relevance of meeting and doubt the potential benefits to their curricula. But by framing how the approach might already build on existing work rather than generating lots of new (sustainability is a theme that readily extends across sciences, engineering and social sciences disciplines), and by highlighting how living labs improve students' employment prospects, sceptical minds can be eased.

So far, the focus at Leicester has been campus wide, but there are plans to extend living lab work into the local community. The city has recently launched a chapter of Citizens UK, a community-organising charity that mobilises universities, faith communities and other civil society organisations to act together for power, social justice and the common good. The chapter at Leicester has been conducting a wide range of listening exercises to raise issues and to identify needs facing the community. It could be that living lab projects become a means to address some of these.

Whilst the idea of university communities mobilising to make a difference may not be new, the living lab approach provides a helpful strategic frame for such work, enabling its institutionalisation.

14 Live projects

Related to

18 Design agency
19 Vertically integrated projects
3 'Traditional' and 4 'critical' service learning

In the field

Birmingham City University
Oxford Brookes University
University of Sheffield

Typical assessment

Group report
Group or individual presentation
Reflective diary

Further reading

Anderson, J (2017) Devising an inclusive and flexible taxonomy of international live projects. *ARENA Journal of Architectural Research*, 2(1). doi:10.5334/ajar.5

Anderson, J & Priest, C (2017) Following John Hejduk's Fabrications: On imagination and reality in the architectural design process. *Architectural Research Quarterly*, 21(2), pp 183–192

Dodds, M, Charlesworth, E & Harrison, F (eds) (2012) *Live Projects: Designing with People*. Melbourne: RMIT University Press

Harriss, H & Widder, L (eds) (2014) *Architecture Live Projects: Pedagogy into Practice*. London: Routledge

See also

The Live Projects Network: https://liveprojectsnetwork.org
Design for Common Good: www.designforcommongood.net
Oxford Brookes University: www.ob1live.org
University of Sheffield: www.liveprojects.org

Summary

Live projects are also referred to variously as design build projects, live build projects, real projects and sometimes as service learning. They're essentially project-based learning experiences, comprising the negotiation of a brief, timescale and budget management and often some form of product development. They provide students with real-life learning experience with an external collaborator. They're commonly found in architectural education, though within this field, projects can vary greatly, often responding to local conditions and the needs of the curriculum. Live projects can range from a permanent building designed and built by students, through to a masterplan designed by students but developed through participatory processes with stakeholders. There are many forms of venture which sit within the live project methodology from small-scale projects, meeting development needs for users that would otherwise be un-met by conventional professional arrangements to medium-scale initiatives which provide some form of permanent habitation, responsive projects, for example, addressing primary human needs in the face of conflict or natural disaster, through to interventionist programmes linked to activism. Often connected with participatory, collaborative, interdisciplinary and sometimes disruptive education methodologies, live projects can also be associated with professional training and construction education and are typically used as a pedagogic means to extend the institutional confines of the design studio. Like some of the other case studies presented in this handbook, we found instances where live projects had been vertically integrated within the curriculum, with students working together

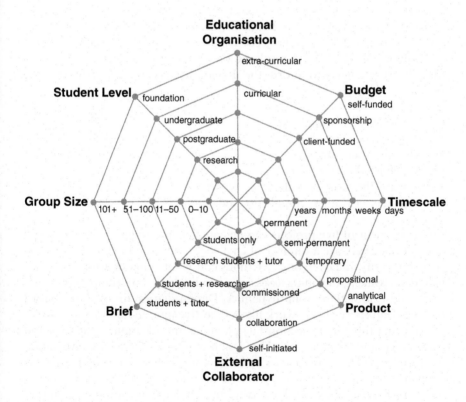

Figure 6.1 Spectrum of live project factors

across year groups. In their analysis, Anderson and Priest (2017) developed a typology that captures this variability of live projects in form.

If the practice of architecture were to fall into two camps, one that focused on aesthetics and the other towards ideological agitation, live projects would sit firmly in the latter (Harriss, 2014). They're the staging ground whereby imagination and reality collide as part of the architectural design process. Where the methodology has favour within architectural schools, it's due in part to its potential to promote understanding in students of the relationship between people and buildings and between buildings and their environment and the need to relate buildings and the spaces between them to human needs and scale.

The projects are bountiful and diverse. Colleagues at Oxford Brookes University cited students working with communities to design and build playable buildings (interactive buildings that are large enough for one person to perform in), developing proposals for a small local museum and outside play spaces combined with weather stations for a local nursery. These projects can all be seen on OB1 Live (www.ob1live.org), a website featuring live projects commissioned by local community groups and designed by students at the Oxford Brookes School of Architecture since 2008.

A number of principles underpin the design of live projects; these were reviewed for the 2014 Live Projects Symposium by Harriet Harriss, a leading exponent of the field. A resultant manifesto was developed that offered the following criteria to inform the design, delivery and evaluation of live projects.

- Respond to pressing need
- Reward successful failure
- Measure social impact
- Redefine what is valuable
- Reward the missing skills
- Engender criticality, complexity and conflict

The assessment of live projects can be complex and requires creativity and innovation. There are a number of challenges, which take time and experience to identify and overcome. Methods consist of a mix of group and individual assessment, including assessing an individual's contribution to group work and role within group dynamics. Design diaries are used at Oxford Brookes University. These work like a reflective journal but are more structured, using three main sections: 1) planning and ideation, 2) actions and steps taken and 3) reflection. The design diaries are used in conversation with students to review progress and ensure it isn't just a record of what has happened on a project but the learning that takes place. There are limitations in what can be assessed formally, and often the methods don't capture the interpersonal learning and transformative aspects of live projects.

Our respondents indicated that live projects require a significant investment in time and resource to manage. Whilst students are involved in this process, too, the extra investment in relationship building, designing and shaping briefs and managing risk can be very demanding, and is often taken over and above the day job. However, with these demands come incredible rewards. One contributor observed that "live projects beautifully connect my teaching, practice and research. They are themselves a form of applied research."

Live projects do indeed straddle the worlds of education, research, practice and society. They offer an alternative pedagogical strategy to more conventional education, which can be isolated from society, self-referential and elitist. The approach is indicative of a shift in architectural practices away from the finished building or place towards the processes of development and the benefits that architectural skillsets can bring to a project. Live projects are by their nature responsive; they meaningfully connect the local with the global and build resilience in communities (and graduates as part of those communities) to issues and crises facing the world today.

15 Placements

Related to

12 Field courses
3 'Traditional' and 4 'critical' service learning
11 Consultancy and client-led briefs

In the field (where to find examples)

University of Hertfordshire
University of Huddersfield
University of Wolverhampton

Typical assessment

Reflective practice
Critical incident analysis
Project work

Further reading

Coldham, S, Flynn, S & Armsby, P (2020) Learning for, at and through work. In H Pokorny & D Warren (eds) *Enhancing Teaching Practice in Higher Education.* London: Sage

See also

Association for Sandwich Education and Training (2017) Good Practice Guide for Work-Based and Placement Learning in Higher Education. Available at: www.asetonline.org/resources/aset-publications/

Summary

Placements belong to the educational tradition of immersion which has been a feature of higher learning in the United Kingdom since the C19th. They represent the primary means by which higher education institutions have attempted to facilitate learning 'in situ', in particular for fields of study that relate to vocations in the mainstream economy. Medicine, teacher education and chaplaincy, for example, all have long traditions of immersing their students directly in practice, so they can 'learn the language' of their vocation, observe the work of experienced colleagues and begin to test and refine their own approaches under supervision.

Placements are best understood as periods of learning experience where students operate under the authority of an employing organisation, which can be in any field or sector. Learning can be captured in various ways in workplace settings and reflected upon when the student returns to their university home. The university remains the primary place of learning in this mode. Placements are related to, but clearly distinguishable from, apprenticeship models – where the primary learning space is the workplace – and approaches to practical work where external stakeholders are invited into the university itself. Placements are time bound but can be imagined as regular commitments, perhaps a certain number of hours or days per week, or extended periods of experience – a week, month or even a year.

The notion of a sandwich placement, normally six months to one year, has been common in the United Kingdom since the growth of polytechnic universities in the 1970s. Sandwich placements are typically located between the second and third years of a degree and give students the opportunity to develop a deep understanding of practice as well as enhancing their transferable skills. As with shorter placements, sandwich years may carry credit and will be assessed in a variety of ways – from reflective practice to skills audits, project work, presentations and critical analysis of particular incidents and events. ASET, the Work Based and Placement Learning Association, has existed for over 30 years in order to support academic and professional support staff working in these areas and continues to generate resources of great value for those looking to develop these forms of learning. Formerly known as the Association for Sandwich Education and Training (ASET), the scope of ASET's work now reflects a much broader range of placements in the sector than simply sandwich placements.

Universities from both research and teaching-intensive sectors utilise placements. Our example comes from the University of Hertfordshire, a teaching-intensive university with a heavy emphasis on applied and multidisciplinary fields such as health, nursing, midwifery, sport, pharmacy, physiotherapy and education. Hertfordshire offers students placements at all levels, from foundation degrees to postgraduate provision. The placements are offered in a variety of modes and are tailored to the particular needs of the field of study. Good practice and resources are shared across the institution, but there's no 'one size fits all' or generic mode of delivery.

The first category of placement at Hertfordshire is the 'practice placement', which reflects a statutory requirement of the particular profession associated with the degree programme. The specifications for the placement are set by the regulatory or accrediting body and are usually delivered in the form of blocks of time throughout the degree. Forms of assessment may also be obligatory, and the University has to comply with a range of quality measures set externally. Degree courses with more autonomy from external regulations may choose between shorter and sandwich placements and have greater freedom with the design of assessment regimes. Shorter placements will typically comprise 30–50 hours of activity in the first year, set within 15 credit modules, rising to 200 or more hours in the third year, in 30 credit or double modules.

In most modules, students experience preparatory or training elements before they enter the placement itself. This is likely to prepare them for the challenges of the workplace but also structure their learning, for example, by encouraging the use of regular reflection. In some degree programmes, for example, sport, professional qualifications are integrated into modules to ensure that students have licence to practice in the field. A sports coach at Hertfordshire would, for example, be able to secure a coaching qualification in a relevant sport before utilising these skills in the workplace or community. As students progress through the levels, they can acquire more advanced qualifications and can take on more responsibility for leadership or delivery.

Assessment of placements at most institutions tends to centre on reflective practice and portfolio building. However, at Hertfordshire, there's greater variation, with the traditions and cultures of different fields of knowledge leading to a range of interpretations. Some degrees, for example health, utilise a version of a portfolio in the form of a practice assessment document, whereas others including engineering, utilise critical incident analysis, deploying language and epistemological approaches familiar to students operating in that particular terrain. Other fields use poster presentations, project reports or skills gap analyses, while some attempt to link the assessment of placements directly to research endeavours in final-year projects.

Although in some instances academic staff at Hertfordshire manage the administrative element of placements, in most cases, they're supported by professional staff in teaching departments and the careers service, who oversee the management of risk, the appointment of mentors, application processes and relationships between the university and external providers. The provision of a substantial placement portfolio, typified by the Hertfordshire approach, requires an infrastructure and appropriately trained, expert staff.

In summary, placements can be used in virtually all degree programmes. They can facilitate learning that enhances employability and develops confidence and networks or that enables students to apply their disciplinary knowledge and develop critical thinking skills. While they are perhaps most commonly associated with business or management fields, the tradition of service learning (see Case Studies 3 and 4) shows us that they can be used to develop thinking in a wide range of disciplines with radically different values and aspirations.

16 Curation

Related to

2 Public engagement
8 Participatory arts
6 Event management

In the field (where to find examples)

University of Sheffield
Goldsmiths, University of London
Bath Spa University

Typical assessment

Reflective practice
Event evaluation
Presentation

Further reading

Montgomery, C (2015) Voices of the bottle kilns: Oral history in Stoke on Trent. In B Stone (ed) *Engaged Learning Sheffield*. Sheffield: The University of Sheffield.

Summary

We take curation to mean the various ways in which knowledge, culture, science and related exhibits and artefacts are presented and translated to public audiences. Historically, curation is associated with the management of civic institutions such as museums, art galleries and libraries. It's reflected in the practices associated with delivering exhibitions, talks, collections, festivals and events. As technology has developed, new forms of knowledge and data have entered circulation, and as a result, conceptions of curation have entered new fields and sectors.

Higher education has a long tradition of educating and training curators. In part, this is related to the mission of institutions to interpret knowledge in order to inform wider publics and the ways in which university collections have been shared and exhibited. Universities across the United Kingdom continue to encourage public access to their libraries and museums. It also relates to the emergence of curators as an occupational group during the course of the C20th. Historically, individuals with responsibilities for curation would have qualifications in art history, archaeology, anthropology or classics. Since the 1990s, and the diversification of subjects and courses that has characterised provision since, curation has become a field of knowledge in its own right. Undergraduate and postgraduate degree courses in curation are now offered at 20 UK institutions. Typically, these courses have some sort of applied element, from work placements with curating organisations to project-based work where students curate particular displays, exhibitions or events in association with industry partners.

While students in these courses develop a wide range of skills that inform the practice of curation, we note that aspects of this process can also be deployed by students in other disciplines and subject areas. The process of analysing, presenting and interpreting knowledge, artefacts or displays for public consumption and benefit can apply to virtually any field. The key to this kind of opportunity is the establishment of an effective partnership with an agency that owns or has access to resources and is willing to allow and enable students to engage with their production processes.

Our example of the curation process comes from the BA English language and linguistics degree at the University of Sheffield. Here, colleagues were frustrated with the tendency for linguistics, in particular, to be taught in an abstract way. There were, it was felt, few opportunities for students to engage directly with spoken data and to apply their learning to the most common forms of language. A 20-credit, single-semester second-year module, A Sense of Place – Local and Regional Identity, addressed this challenge by working with external agencies in order to enable students to engage with archives of the spoken word and to use their technical and research skills to analyse dialects and their context.

In the past five years, the module has engaged a number of external partners, but the relationship with the greatest impact has been with the Gladstone Pottery Museum in Stoke-on-Trent. The Gladstone rediscovered a large oral history that had been collected in locality in the early 2000s but didn't have the internal resources to edit and present the material. Instead, it worked with academic colleagues at Sheffield to develop an opportunity for students to engage in the process of producing excerpts for public consumption, allowing museum visitors to listen to a unique historical account of the area in the voices of local people. Thousands of visitors have subsequently listened to the excerpts in their tours of the museum, and several cohorts of students have been able to interact directly with recordings of the Stoke-on-Trent dialect.

The module is organised around two strands of activity. The first centres on theoretical concepts and contemporary research and is delivered in an essentially conventional way. The second focuses on the process of editing and presenting the archive. Small teams of four or five students are formed in order to work on this aspect. The teams are allocated themes, relating to historical or cultural aspects of the Stoke-on-Trent area, and a set of related episodes from the archives. The students then work collectively in order to create two or three short excerpts of up to a minute, with the aim of contributing them to the ongoing exhibition at the museum. Staff at the museum establish criteria against which the excerpts are judged and which determine whether they're eventually put on display. The criteria allow for some interpretation and creativity on the part of the students, but the final output has to be suitable for the exhibition.

Students use freely available editing software to interact with the archive and publish their work as digital files. The work is shared initially at a module conference, where the teams, staff and external stakeholders gather to hear the material and to listen to the students explain their rationale for the approach taken. The students are then assessed in relation to their presentation at the conference and through a sample of their reflections from a journal which they complete fortnightly, via the university virtual learning environment, throughout the process.

All stakeholders attest to the success of the module. Students see the value of connecting 'real world' examples to abstract theory and produce consistently positive module evaluations. External agencies see genuine benefit from the partnership and can add value to their collections at minimal cost while ensuring the quality of the artefacts presented. Although the Sheffield example is relatively unusual, we see great potential for this approach to be adopted more widely. The widespread archiving of digital data presents all kinds of opportunities for students to extend their involvement in the analysis, organisation and presentation of knowledge for public good.

17 Legacy projects

Related to

22 Student action
2 Public engagement
21 STEAM

In the field

Cardiff University

Typical assessment

Pitch or presentation
Resource production
Reflective practice

Further reading

Rutherford, S M & Prytherch, Z (2016) Assessment 'for' learning: Students support-ing the learning of their peers through the development of multimedia learning resources. In D Simoes & M Pinheiro (eds) *Handbook of Research on Engaging Digital Natives in Higher Education Settings*. Hershey, PA: IGI Global. pp 121–153
Scott, J, Moxham, B & Rutherford, S (2013) Building an open academic environment – A new approach to empowering students in their learning of anatomy through 'shadow modules.' *Anatomy*, 224(30), pp 286–295

Summary

Legacy projects are typically forms of group work or assessments that ena-ble students to create learning resources for their peers. The resources can be traditional, in the sense that they can be in the form of academic papers or presentations, or they can reflect more contemporary information and communication technologies. There are two broad aims for legacy projects. The first is to engage students in the process of articulating, communicating and presenting core concepts so that they better understand content in their field. The second is to engage students with an assessment activity in which the output of their work is directly beneficial to the student and their peers rather than the benefit simply deriving from feedback on a specified skill. Legacy projects are founded on the maxim that 'the best way to learn is to teach' and that those with the greatest exposure to the contemporary ver-nacular are most likely to produce effective means of communication with student communities.

Legacy projects can be created for learners in many different contexts – so for peers in a learning community, for those in other year groups or even for learners in other educational layers or systems. In this sense, legacy projects can be seen to be related to public engagement (see Case Study 2) and the idea of relaying theoretical concepts and advances to different publics and communities, but a key distinction is the desire of legacy projects to be archived and to contribute to a body of knowledge that can be deployed in the longer term. Legacy projects that incorporate multimedia approaches can be easily stored and shared and act as supportive materials for cohorts of learners beyond the current setting. This form of work also relates to peer learning approaches, which can be utilised within or beyond the formal curriculum, and to student-as-producer approaches and the notion that engagement is heightened where learners enjoy more choice, control and collaboration and the ability to be creative.

Our case study comes from the School of Biosciences at Cardiff University. The school has a long-standing commitment to peer-assisted learning and has for some time supported the idea of 'shadow modules', where staff and students work together to form a face-to-face or online learning community that shares understanding and interpretation. Shadow modules operate alongside the standard, formal delivery, and although co-ordination is provided by staff members, it's volunteer students who lead collaborative endeavours and also occasionally produce resources that support the formal curriculum. This wider culture of staff–student partnership has supported the development of legacy projects within taught provision, specifically as part of the second-year cell biology module, a year-long, double module that considers and explores fundamental concepts in the field.

Students in the module engage with content in a traditional format at the outset but are then set an independent project to produce a learning resource for revision purposes for their peers. The project is scheduled from November to March, enabling resources to be evaluated, refined, assessed and published in time for the summer revision/examination period. Students are placed into project groups of five or six and are then allocated concepts or topics from the curriculum (for example, cell membrane structure, structure and function of the mitochondria, import and export of proteins). No more than two groups are given the same topic to work with. Training and scaffolding are provided for the groups, but they're then expected to work independently to produce the resource over the five-month period.

An assessment-for-learning approach is deployed so that the structure of assignments supports the production of the resources. First, the student groups present their resource to their peers and to staff, demonstrating its utility and discussing the rationale behind the development, as well as affordances and limitations for learning. This presentation forms the first part of the assessment. The groups act on feedback elicited at this point and then submit their refined resource for assessment. Criteria at this point include coverage of the subject matter, accuracy and clarity, ease of use of resource and the degree of challenge shown in production. Students then also collaborate to produce a reflective account of their team experiences using a collaborative document platform and also submit peer assessment reports to assist staff in moderation activities.

Students consistently employ new and developing technologies in the production of their resources. Narrated PowerPoint presentations, videos, animations, Prezi presentations, online quizzes, websites, YouTube resources, wikis, smartphone apps, eBooks, blogs and podcasts have all featured consistently in the past few years, with new adaptations evident in the work of every cohort. Hard-copy resources, in more traditional formats, can be submitted, but most work is created and stored electronically. Current and past work is stored on a wiki, accessible to all within the university, with an outward-facing website also in production. Thus, the assessment produces an extensive resource bank, using a diversity of media that caters to differences in learning preferences, that students can use to support their learning.

The benefits of the legacy project at Cardiff are wide ranging. Students report that they enjoy the variation in assessment, and a healthy proportion of each cohort uses the resources for their revision purposes as well as learning through the production process. Staff value the opportunity to learn from – and on occasion be inspired by – the students and also recognise the value of legacy projects in building skills for collaboration, digital literacy and employability. Students tend to opt for higher-risk approaches, experimenting with approaches initially unfamiliar to them, but consistently succeed in achieving high marks and producing resources of great quality. The diversity of media utilised by the students pleasantly surprises staff on an annual basis.

Legacy projects are utilised at Cardiff in a science, technology, engineering and mathematics setting, but the approach could be usefully deployed in any field, with resources produced for peers in the same year group or for a wide range of alternative learning communities.

18 Design agency

Related to

11 Consultancy and client-led briefs
9 Trading entities
19 Vertically integrated projects

In the field

University of Edinburgh
Falmouth University
Arts University Bournemouth

Typical assessment

Reflective diaries
Presentations
Blogs

Further reading

Logan, C D (2006) Circles of practice: Educational and professional graphic design. *Journal of Workplace Learning*, 18(6), pp 331–343

Patterson, Z (2018a) Design agencies within university and designers in residence within school. *A Paper Presented to 12th International Technology, Education and Development Conference*, Valencia, Spain, 5–7 March. Available at: https://library.iated.org/view/PATTERSON2018DES (Accessed: 23 January 2020)

Patterson, Z (2018b) Design agency: 100% employable. *Teaching Matters Blog*, 7 June. University of Edinburgh. Available at: www.teaching-matters-blog.ed.ac.uk/design-agency-100-employable/ (Accessed: 23 January 2020)

Summary

Our case study – design agency – comes from the BA (Hons) graphic design programme at Edinburgh College of Art, University of Edinburgh, and is the flagship means by which students in the programme can graduate from four years' full-time education with an honours degree whilst simultaneously garnering four years' work experience. Developed some 14 years ago, design agency is the model through which specialist learning undertaken in graphic design classrooms is applied to industry practices and vice versa. The first project of its kind in the United Kingdom, it was winner of the Employability Initiative category in the 2013 Guardian University Awards.

To best prepare graduates for industry, design agency is delivered through both an innovative structure and carefully conceived student roles that facilitate vertical integration (i.e. students working across year groups) in the graphic design programme. Through a 40-credit, year-long course, around

20 fourth-year undergraduate students take on creative director roles, forming between five and nine design agencies which operate as profit-generating companies. Creative directors brand and advertise vacancies at various points throughout the academic year as follows:

- *Interns:* First-year students recruited as part of an elective, 20-credit design agency module for semester two;
- *Junior designers:* Second-year students recruited as part of an elective, 20-credit design agency module for semester one;
- *Senior designers:* Third-year students recruited as part of a core, 20-credit design agency module for semester two.

Alongside these roles, established design professionals (an increasing number of whom are graduates of the design agency project themselves) provide voluntary mentorship. Mentors are sourced by creative directors to ensure that they match the particular ethos and values of the design agency in question.

The innovative way of structuring the programme across year groups, semesters and core versus elective modules has a multitude of benefits. With their teams changing throughout the year, creative directors are challenged by managing different skillsets, characters and dynamics. Occasionally, the course convenor throws in additional challenges for creative directors – for example, managing the redundancy of a senior designer – to prevent things becoming too predictable and to test their ability to deal with the unexpected, albeit within the safe testing ground of an academic environment.

The vertical integration of the course design means that, regardless of age or experience, but based on ability, students work collectively towards a common objective. And peer feedback and support emerge naturally between the year groups with, for example, fourth-year students often advising first-year students on their portfolios.

As students progress through design agency, differing learning outcomes are met, all converging on the aim that, through work-like scenarios, students develop rounded, 'real world' skillsets. Broadly, learning outcomes at each stage are:

Interns:

- Demonstrate understanding of classic design agency structures and methods of working;
- Reflect upon role as an intern within a group context;
- Communicate personal direction and career plan to an audience.

Junior designers:

- Explore multiple design agency structures and various methods of working;

- Reflect upon role and contribution as a junior designer within a group context;
- Employ appropriate methods for communicating personal direction and career plan to an audience.

Senior designers:

- Demonstrate understanding of the range of professional graphic design agency roles and responsibilities;
- Reflect upon role and contribution as a senior designer within a group context;
- Communicate a long-term career strategy to an audience.

Creative directors:

- Manage and motivate others within a group setting;
- Reflect upon role and contribution as a creative director;
- Communicate a short-term and long-term career strategy to an audience.

Achievement against learning outcomes is assessed through a range of reflective documentation – diaries, blogs, films, pecha kucha presentations and the like. Year groups always keep reflective diaries about their work and roles, reflecting on occasionally bumpy rides, and these generally account for 50% of the total course mark. Assessment techniques for the remaining 50% vary dependent on year group, with, for example, fourth-year students producing publications that highlight their key learning points and professional and personal impacts from the course and second-year students producing a visual artefact about a key learning experience.

For the professionals that offer voluntary mentorship, design agency redresses industry concerns over graduate readiness for work. Practically, it helps mentors to see students in action before any potential recruitment further down the line. And the students also provide a ready source of unpaid interns to cover for staff sickness, holidays and the like that may occasionally hit mentor-providing agencies.

For students, the real value lies in the long-term relationships built through a variety of mentors and peers from up to four different teams. Through these relationships, and through increasing levels of responsibility and workload as they progress through design agency, students develop their confidence, their networks, their understanding of their strengths and their future career goals. They develop a new understanding of self, often reimagining their career paths in the process.

Through continued innovations – the course has recently opened to students outside of graphic design, enabling an interdisciplinary mix – and through maintenance of its considered curricula structure, design agency will persist in challenging students in new ways so as to better prepare them for the world of work.

19 Vertically integrated projects

Related to

14 Live projects
2 Public engagement
18 Design agency

In the field

University of Strathclyde
University of St Andrews

Typical assessment

Logbook or diary
Peer evaluations
Project report

Further reading

Coyle, E, Allebach, J & Garton, K (2006) The vertically integrated projects (VIP) program in ECE at Purdue: Fully integrating undergraduate education and graduate research. *A Paper Presented to Proceedings of the 2006 ASEE Annual Conference and Exposition*, Chicago, 18–21 June

Strachan, S, Marshall, S, Murray, P, Coyle, E & Sonnenberg-Klein, J (2019) Using vertically integrated projects to embed research-based education for sustainable development in undergraduate curricula. *International Journal of Sustainability in Higher Education*, 20(8), pp 1313–1328

Summary

Vertically integrated projects (VIPs) are forms of group work that allow students from all year groups to work shoulder to shoulder with research students and experienced research staff. VIPs focus on long-term research projects, sustaining the interest of individual students as they progress through the curriculum. Students typically work within the parameters of a single VIP in the second, third, and in some cases fourth years of their undergraduate degree and may also progress through masters stages, with some extending their studies even further through PhD programmes.

VIPs are an example of research-engaged provision and enable students to use their scholarship skills to directly address real world problems. By breaking with the tendency to organise groups horizontally, within year groups, VIPs enable more experienced students to mentor others while allowing all participants to develop understanding of career pathways in research. They also overcome some of the challenges of modularised systems where students compartmentalise knowledge and struggle to build effectively on their learning. The final distinguishing feature of VIPs is their interdisciplinarity, and although they can be organised within single fields or courses, they're most effective when they welcome contributions from students with divergent expertise.

VIPs are common in the United States and growing in popularity across the globe. The Georgia Institute of Technology has for some time led the way in the field and now offers an outstanding array of VIPs for students to choose from. Long-standing VIPs have made significant innovations and impacts, generated substantial external funding and led to jointly authored research outputs. In the United Kingdom, Strathclyde has had the most notable success and organises its VIPs around either staff or institutional research interests, which also match the priorities identified in the United Nations' Sustainable Development Goals.

At both Georgia Tech and Strathclyde, VIPs number between 10 and 20 undergraduates and up to four postgraduate students, representing a range of specialisms. The students go through a competitive application process (not necessarily based on academic record) to join the projects and then work under the supervision of the project lead and ultimately the VIP director, normally a senior academic. Students typically join VIPs in their second year, having engaged with foundational knowledge before making their decision to apply. They then continue over a three-year period, often until graduation or their point of departure. The VIPs are housed within dedicated modules with appropriate levels of credit. At Strathclyde, students engage on a year-round basis via two ten-credit modules (one in each semester), but clearly 'long-thin' or higher-credit modules could be deployed where institutional frameworks allow.

Assessment occurs at the middle and end of each semester. It centres on reflective devices such as logs or diaries and then elements related to outputs such as posters, presentations and reports. An extensive peer evaluation process is conducted in order to account for variable contributions to groups. Learning is often shared through celebratory events or conferences, and at Strathclyde, an annual VIP Festival is organised by event management students. As individuals progress through their degrees, they take on different roles within the team, developing their collaborative skills while making significant technical contributions. Exposure to VIPs enables students to integrate within research and subject communities, and many go on to pursue MSc or PhD programmes that otherwise would not have been contemplated.

VIPs enable students to develop their research skills, confidence and teamworking capabilities and give a sense of agency and engagement. Demand for access is high, and satisfaction rates are understandably positive. They're also of considerable value to staff and to the institution, creating enthusiastic, responsive and imaginative teams of students who commit to long-term participation in data collection, analysis, design and innovation. VIPs create a space where different departments and interests can collaborate and can call on expertise from professional service departments, alumni and external stakeholders and publics. They're therefore agile, flexible and permeable, allowing knowledge to flow through the walls of the university.

Topics for VIPs are identified by academics or, once a team is underway, via collaboration with the teams themselves. They tend not to accept propositions from external interests, as in the case of Grand Challenges, as this can restrict the agency of staff or students. Examples of VIPs at Strathclyde include Robotic Vehicles for Education and Research, Text Lab (which uses computer programmes to analyse Shakespearian plays), Water and Sanitation Hygiene, Drug Discovery and Sustainable Energy for Development. Projects have delivered innovations in the United Kingdom and Africa and led to substantial advances in collaboration, research and innovation.

Most VIPs are focused on research engagement and are therefore particularly well suited to STEM institutions or research-intensives. However, the same mode could in principle be deployed in programmes where a practice orientation was more prominent or where extensive networks of placements required greater support or sustainability.

20 Product development

Related to

18 Design agency
11 Consultancy and client-led briefs
7 Business clinics

In the field (where to find examples)

Cardiff Metropolitan University
University of Central Lancashire
University of Bradford

Typical assessment

Portfolio
Observed practice
Pitch or presentation

Further reading

Healey, M, Lannin, L, Stibbe, A & Derounian, J (2013) *Developing and Enhancing Undergraduate Final-Year Projects and Dissertations.* York: The Higher Education Academy.
Wrigley, C & Straker, K (2017) Design thinking pedagogy: The educational design ladder. *Innovations in Education and Teaching International*, 54(4), pp 374–385

Summary

Product development is a feature of higher education courses that incorporate the design, building and testing of artefacts for use in industrial, commercial or everyday settings. It's deployed most obviously in engineering contexts but also in business, computer science and technology-related fields. The methods utilised in product development reflect the body of knowledge that has developed in secondary and tertiary education around product design and centre on conception, analysis and various stages of synthesis, including ideation, implementation and evaluation. Although the aims and underpinning philosophies may differ, product development reflects some of the features and approaches commonly associated with fields in the creative arts. Product development can be carried out by individuals or, more commonly in university settings, in groups. Typically an external partner, organisation or community will be involved in delivery and will represent the client or consumer of the product in question.

Our case focuses on a suite of optional product development modules in the BSc food science and technology course at Cardiff Metropolitan University. The modules represent excellent practice in their own right, but, as we'll see, they're the basis for an unusual university-wide collaboration which points the way towards all kinds of exciting possibilities for future innovation. In their original form, the second-year New Product Development and third-year New Product Development 2 offer students the chance to take their own product from conception to launch, to test and stretch their collaborative skills and to work directly with industry partners. Both modules are worth 20 credits and run for a single semester.

In the second-year module, product briefs are prepared by food production companies, and students work in groups of four in order to respond to industry requirements. Ideas are developed through six practical sessions, with staff on hand to support discussion and testing. The resultant food product is developed in purpose-built kitchens on campus and includes consideration of shelf life, labelling, packaging and legal issues. Prototypes are presented at a Product Development Fair, and industry partners contribute to feedback and formative assessment. In their third year, students essentially follow the same process but are given greater responsibility and independence. Product briefs at this stage are negotiated rather than specified, with the participants working individually or in smaller groups. Additionally, students have to take account of sustainability issues and ensure that issues relating to food security and environmental impact are considered.

Assessment of these modules takes three forms. First, students produce individual product history portfolios, detailing the various stages of development and explaining decision-making processes. Second, students make Dragons Den–style presentations, seeking support from stakeholders in the form of role-playing lecturers. Finally, the performance of students as technicians and collaborators is observed by lecturers in the practical kitchen spaces. Staff interview students to supplement their observations, enabling them to monitor progress in situ. Students are able to complete the production process and see their consumers interact with the product, but the process also affords students the opportunity to learn from decisions or mistakes and to act in an enterprising manner when appropriate.

Evaluations indicate consistently high levels of satisfaction from students on the modules, and many attest to wide-ranging benefits in relation to their employability. However, in 2018, the story of the modules took a new twist when the former Welsh rugby union international and filmmaker, Richard Parks, contacted the course team to ask if students could design and produce food products to support his attempt to break the world record for a solo journey to the South Pole. Second-year students were immediately put to work through the modules, designing freeze-dried meals and snacks to fuel Richard's hazardous and exhausting journey. It was anticipated that he would require 7,000 calories a day, with 1,000-calorie meals supplemented by 400-calorie snacks. Working closely with Richard and his team, the students prototyped and refined various options before using specialised equipment in the Cardiff Metropolitan kitchens to produce a range of items – including a freeze-dried two-course Christmas dinner – that were shipped to South America, air-freighted to the Antarctic and then consumed on the trip.

At the same time, academic colleagues in other departments at the university also set to work on projects that would contribute to the world-record attempt. Students in art and design, computer science and media worked in final-year project modules in order to build and deliver Richard's sledge, to design and build a robot that collected environmental samples from the Antarctic setting and to deliver a range of media resources in order to capture learning from the partnership. Although, ultimately, Richard was unsuccessful in his world-record attempt – he was undone by freak weather conditions – the whole project was seen by all partners as an enormous success. The process was repeated in the years that followed, with Richard pursuing different physical and mental challenges each time.

The Cardiff Metropolitan case offers us inspiration on many counts and also suggests ways in which students from a range of fields and courses might contribute to specific university projects or challenges. In this instance, the collaboration is based on students working within their specialism, brought together either by an external partner or by a central co-ordinating function or person. Alternatively, students could come together to attack the challenges, forming multidisciplinary teams or collaborations through their final-year project work.

21 STEAM

Related to

8 Participatory arts
18 Design agency
10 Applied theatre

In the field

King's College London
Oxford Brookes University
Queen's University Belfast

Typical assessment

Reflective journals
Podcasts, vlogs
Presentations

Further reading

Segarra, V A, Natalizio, B, Falkenberg, C V, Pulford, S & Holmes, R M (2018) STEAM: Using the arts to train well-rounded and creative scientists. *Journal of Microbiology & Biology Education*, 19(1). doi:10.1128/jmbe.v19i1.1360

Smyth Zahra, F (2018) Clinical humanities: Informal, transformative learning opportunities, where knowledge gained from humanities epistemologies is translated back into clinical practice, supporting the development of professional autonomy in undergraduate dental students. *MedEdPublish*. doi:10.15694/mep.2018.0000163.2

Veen, M, Skelton, J & de la Croix, A (2020) Knowledge, skills and beetles: Respecting the privacy of private experiences in medical education. *Perspectives on Medical Education*. doi:10.1007/s40037-020-00565-5

Summary

STEAM pedagogy – the acronym standing for science, technology, engineering, arts and mathematics – involves an infusion of creativity, by means of the arts, into the education and training of future scientists (Segarra et al., 2018). In such endeavours, the most common art form used is the visual arts, as, after all, most scientists have to generate diagrams to communicate their science effectively. But there's also a role for the performative arts, the likes of dance and theatre, in science and clinical education.

Whichever art form is used, STEAM pedagogy recognises the value of art not as a simple vehicle for scientific content but as a valid contributor, facilitating environments where transformative learning can arise. Such learning is crucial to driving the professional identity formation and personal development of students, promoting new ways of thinking, to take risks and to challenge previously held assumptions, reflecting about 'becoming' a professional.

Our example is taken from the Faculty of Dentistry, Oral & Craniofacial Sciences at King's College London. *Thriving in Cultural London* is a compulsory, semester-long module undertaken by 130 first-year bachelor of dental surgery students. This interactive, participatory arts-based learning module sees the students immersed in London's cultural offering through a series of eight three-hour-long activity sessions.

The University's Culture team collaborated with the faculty to develop these sessions with a range of cultural partners. Activities are diverse, covering a multitude of art forms – from trips to Sadler's Wells Theatre to participant observation at Tate Modern, from a beginner's contemporary dance workshop with Ballet Rambert to freewriting in the Undercroft skatepark and more. Alongside these opportunities, students are challenged to identify their own cultural highlights of London, creating walking tours both for their classmates and an imaginary 'other' (e.g. a small child or someone with a visual impairment) so as to test their caring abilities. All activities encourage students to become curious explorers of the city, to observe, engage, delve deeper – elements of being a good dentist.

A new offering from the faculty as of 2019, a core aim of the module is to help students transition to university life by promoting student wellbeing, fostering community and enabling students to build a sense of belonging. The transition to university is a period of significant personal change, and a sense of belongingness can help reduce rates of anxiety, depression and burnout and address ethnicity attainment gaps. Simply, a sense of belonging enables students to engage with their vulnerabilities, to try new ideas and step outside of their comfort zone – that is, to partake in the transformative learning where most personal growth and the progression to 'becoming' professional can occur.

As such, *Thriving in Cultural London* aims to curate transformative learning environments that may help students accept their vulnerability and become more tolerant of both risk and ambiguity. It's also designed to instil early leadership attributes and to encourage self-awareness, reflexivity and reflective practice. Students are given journals and encouraged to jot down their thoughts throughout the sessions, to reflect and to note ideas and observations. Their reflections are also prompted by a range of questions, such as:

- What do you understand by culture(s)?
- What do you value about your own culture?
- What do you think *Thriving in Cultural London* might have to offer you?

Alongside journals, students summed up at the end of the module what they felt they'd learnt about themselves and others and about cultures in London, encouraging self-awareness and reflexivity. In addition, as part of the evaluation strategy, the pilot cohort completed the Harvard Flourishing Measure survey (https://hfh.fas.harvard.edu/files/pik/files/flourishing_measure_pdf.pdf) at commencement and at the end of the academic year. This survey is designed to assess various domains of wellbeing – happiness and life satisfaction, mental and physical health, meaning and purpose, character and virtue, close social relationships and financial and material stability – and helps students illuminate their lived experiences and development through the module.

Students have observed that an exploration of their surroundings prompts an exploration of self and that London is full of stories, different cultures and values, just like their future patients and colleagues. Dentistry is a demanding, stressful career. In building empathy, cultural agility and adaptability, and in encouraging students to be curious and take risks without fearing failure, *Thriving in Cultural London* scaffolds students in their professional journeys. As one student reflected, "Exploring your surroundings in turn allows you to engage in an exploration of yourself."

The next iteration of the module will continue to deploy STEAM learning integrated with humanities as a signature pedagogy to support dental students' exploration of self as they acquire their professional identity.

22 Student action

Related to

2 Public engagement
3 'Traditional' service learning
15 Placements

In the field (where to find examples)

Newcastle University
University of Lincoln
University of Winchester

Typical assessment

Reflective practice
Group project
Individual interview/viva

Further reading

Bryson, C (2020) From then to now in student engagement – An academic's perspective. In T Lowe & Y Hakim, Y (eds) *Student Engagement in Higher Education: Theory into Practice*. Abingdon: Routledge
Bryson, C, Brooke, J, Foreman, S, Graham, S & Brayshaw, G (2018) Modes of partnership: Universal, selective, representational and pseudo partnership. *Student Engagement in Higher Education Journal*, 2(1)

See also

The RAISE (Researching, Advancing and Inspiring Student Engagement) Network: www.raise-network.com

Summary

Many of the cases that we've reviewed so far embrace the ideals of social justice and the desire to promote equitable relationships between universities and their stakeholders. Student action reflects these aspirations, but rather than looking to work with and empower local communities or organisations, the aim with this approach is to create situations where students can take ownership of the design, delivery and evaluation of learning processes. There is, obviously, a long history of students engaging in direct action in order to engage with the broader political process, to contribute to debates on higher education or to make representations to their university. Our interest, however, is in the deliberate attempts by institutions to encourage or facilitate this kind of activity in order to improve the learning environment. In some instances, the motive of the institution will be to improve its service by getting closer to its 'consumers'; in others, these desires will have more to do with a constructivist pedagogy which takes seriously what students bring with them and the contributions that they can make. Some academics, furthermore, may be influenced by critical pedagogy and see great value in enabling students to understand their position in relation to those who hold power and to act in ways that build confidence and influence.

The growth of interest in these processes in the past two decades is reflected in the influence and reputation of the RAISE network. RAISE is a broad church which promotes innovation in relation to student voice, student empowerment and 'students as partners' endeavours. It recognises the contributions that students can make to all conceptions and aspects of higher education and attempts to build models of partnership working that can bring benefits to all stakeholders. Much of the work of RAISE relates to activities in the extracurricular realm and attempts to foster change through representative and consultative processes, funded projects and design activities. There are, however, examples of students becoming engaged in this kind of work within the curriculum itself. We consider this work authentic because it affords the opportunity for students to utilise their scholarship for the benefit of others, to tackle issues of genuine concern to themselves and their peers and to make direct and lasting contributions to their immediate environment.

Our example of authentic student action comes from the BA Combined Honours programme at the Newcastle University. The Combined Honours provision is designed to enable students to retain the breadth of approach that they may have enjoyed at school while ensuring that they achieve a depth of understanding befitting a higher education. Students typically choose from a wide range of subjects and select two or three disciplines or fields to study. They'll often choose additionally from a small basket of 'core' options, modules that support them as they make sense of, and synthesise, the diverse knowledge with which they engage and which support future thinking in relation to graduate outcomes, employability or careers planning. Students emerge as interdisciplinarians with capabilities that – it's argued – prepare them effectively for both employment and lifelong learning.

The Combined Honours programme draws from humanities, business, social science and languages and has a track-record of approaches that empower students. All of the core modules in the programme have been co-designed with students, and the programme actively encourages student involvement in representation, peer-assisted learning and mentoring. Some modules embrace co-design on an annual basis, with student groups invited to work alongside lecturing staff to determine content, delivery methods and assessment. The particular example for us is the Graduate Development module, which is a 20-credit option running across both semesters. The year-long format is designed to facilitate deep learning and the sense that students may take some time to process ideas about their political 'position' in an institution and then potential contributions that they might achieve once they embrace their capabilities and agency. The module is available to students in both the second and third years of the degree and generally attracts around 20 students.

The module aims to develop self-awareness, an appreciation of graduate capabilities, collaborative skills and a sense of agency and confidence. It's split into two main components, an individual experience and a group project. In the first half of the module, students focus on a role that they've acquired in relation to the course and its infrastructure. This may be as a peer mentor, peer learning associate, student union society officer, course representative or another related role. The students develop a reflective portfolio as part of their experience and then focus on two areas of personal capability – for example, communication or collaborative skills – in detail for their assessment. In the second half, students form small teams and are charged with the task of developing a proposal, intervention or activity of benefit to their fellow students. A number of strong partnerships have developed in this space, and students have been able to build lasting interventions in relation to representation, feedback, learning resources and student involvement at all levels of course management and delivery. Students are then assessed via a group report and an individual interview.

The success of the Graduate Development module has much to do with the broader culture of student empowerment in the course. Once they reach the module, students have had exposure to interventions aimed at developing partnerships and will have a specific role on which to reflect. The module then affords them the time, space and psychological security to explore new approaches and bring forward imaginative ideas. Staff on the course are proud of the module and its impact but acknowledge that often, in order to enable students to find their voice, they have to 'step back' or 'let go' and that this process can itself be disconcerting and challenging.

Chapter 7

Conclusion

Introduction

Whilst our overall position in this book has been to argue that authentic learning is worth the effort, we don't want to position it as a magic bullet for all the injustices of society, for improving student employability and life chances and for furthering the reputation of your institution. Not only would this be unrealistic and dishonest, to do so would ignore the risks of the approach. There are times when through authentic learning you can do more harm than good. Student experience may not be improved, partners may invest time and get very little in return, the reputation of your institution may get dented.

The approaches we've selected here are representative of many different flavours of authentic learning. There is diversity in discipline focus, in delivery mode, in institution types and in partner organisations, but most importantly, you'll find examples of 'doing to', 'doing for', 'doing with' and 'doing alongside' the other. Whilst doing authentic learning with or alongside partners is often preferable, we've not sought to argue from a particular position, that is, that all authentic learning *must be* or *has to be* by definition delivered alongside partners. We hold a healthy degree of pragmatism about authentic learning, and we know that some programmes will be imbued with unhelpful dynamics of pity, sympathy, misunderstanding or exploitation in both directions.

In seeking to cover a breadth of activity across different project types, we may have missed much by way of detail. This may be frustrating to some readers. We've not looked at authentic learning from a class perspective, we've barely touched upon inclusivity in curriculum design and we've only nodded towards social justice. For several of the case studies that we've included, inclusivity, equality, diversity and social justice are all living and active concerns. They are cornerstones of the approach themselves. However, for other case studies, they are not primary. Rather, skills and employability are foregrounded. We contend that whichever way you come at this, there is always more to learn.

We also acknowledge the lack of student voice throughout the text. Our contacts and respondents were practising academics, all of whom pointed to resources that evaluated the impact of their work on students. We therefore make connections to sources that examine the student experience, but we aren't able to prioritise these voices in our work on this occasion. Readers should be cognisant of this as they assess our contribution.

Critical awareness and reflection on the context of authentic learning are, as we hope we've demonstrated, of paramount importance. As an educator or manager seeking to deploy these approaches, you'll be required to make conscious decisions about the whys and wherefores of authentic learning, to be reflective about power – your institution's power but also your own personal power – and to constantly seek to shift the balance where appropriate towards your students and external partners.

Work within your institution

The institution you're based in – the institutional culture – will have an impact on how easy or difficult it is to get authentic learning off the ground and to sustain projects. We've found that authentic learning can flourish when it is a top-level priority for an institution, and by this, we mean where it is something the institution is committed to developing and nourishing, as signified with investment and the reward and recognition of people involved.

We've visited different institutions at different stages of their development. In some places, we met with lone renegades, who appeared to be working upstream, against the grain. In other institutions, it appeared that someone had lit a tinderbox, and this kind of work was both incredibly visible at a strategic level and seemed to permeate how staff and students spoke about the institution and its place. It had become 'the way' of teaching for the institution, not necessarily adopted by all, but an approach that drew on the distinctive strengths and traditions of the institution. We also visited some places where authentic learning practices had been co-opted unhelpfully by the institution, taking the programme down a path that sat uncomfortably with the people involved – for example, emphasising employability over social justice.

To be legitimised, authentic learning must be seen to be of equal value to traditional academic activities, implemented with critical rigour. It can't be approached in a frivolous or ad-hoc manner. Some of the most exciting examples that emerge from this work are those that form part of a collaborative fabric that is woven throughout an institutional culture and its community. Take, for example, the work on Connected Curriculum at University College London (UCL). The approach is at the core of UCL's education strategy and aims to ensure that all students are able to learn through participating in research and enquiry at all levels of the curriculum.

Similarly, Staffordshire University has adopted the idea of 'the connected university' within its strategic plan. Connecting communities to a digitally led, connected curriculum that features real world learning is a core part of its educational ambition. Whilst both universities have adopted the idea of connectivity, the way it plays out for students and staff is different in each context and is very much flavoured by the priorities, history and, to some extent, the geography of the university and its specific role within that locality. Take another example – Falmouth University, where its strategic mantra is 'doing it for real', underpinned by a commitment to ensure that every student should have a placement opportunity as part of their learning. The focus here is on incubation and enterprise. And whilst the University of Sheffield also has these strands to its activity, it has embraced the concept of 'engaged learning' which speaks to the civic tradition of the university and its role in supporting and working with the communities of Sheffield. Whatever the focus, these high-level strategic drivers create cultures where there is space for authentic learning. They help a university deploy its resources and are often accompanied with appropriate governance structures to ensure quality and innovation.

Where next for authentic learning?

We're acutely aware that our snowball approach to case study sampling means that we'll have missed many wonderful examples of authentic learning. We've managed to highlight good practice, in various ways, at over 50 UK universities and in at least 30 different disciplines or fields of study, but we appreciate that we're only scratching the surface. We hope that we've at least demonstrated the incredible diversity of approaches at different institutions and case studies that are coherent, inspiring and replicable.

There were some approaches that we searched for but were unable to find. While it's clearly possible that they're out there somewhere, we were surprised not to find examples of authentic learning in immersive spaces, such as virtual or enhanced reality. Accepting that some may baulk at notions of authenticity in manufactured realms, what we were looking for were examples of students building environments for others to explore or inhabit or situations where students could leave their own mark on spaces created for them. What we found instead were simulations, particularly in medicine, dentistry, architecture and geography, where students could explore places and spaces that would otherwise be difficult or dangerous – for a variety of stakeholders – to enter. Although there were examples, from Australia and elsewhere, of students building lasting environments in Minecraft scenarios, these were at earlier, primary and secondary stages of learning, not at higher.

Many of these simulated environments were impressive and presented obvious benefits to students, but we didn't include them because ultimately, they failed to fit our criterion of agency, the ability of students to have an impact and shape the world for others. Generally, simulations were problematic because despite their many strengths, they frequently failed to make connections to the real world or to actual practice. A good example of this is the current trend for business and management schools to invest in the building and equipping of trading rooms, which enable students to engage in 'realistic' physical and online environments where they practice the buying and selling of shares and commodities. Although there were many admirable examples of these facilities, students involved essentially engaged in game-playing, with learning episodes controlled by parameters imposed by academics or by trading software. No opportunities here for students to defeat the Kobayashi Maru[1] or simply to spend some actual money, even of nominal value.

Simulations using avatars or Second Life–style interactions could afford students the chance to interact with immersive environments in a more personal and potentially lasting way, but again, we were unable to find examples of this kind of approach. Given the growing permeation of algorithms and machine learning in shaping our experience of the 'real world', the lack of opportunity in education for students to influence, shape or disrupt virtual or programmed worlds is of concern. We're sure there are some out there, and technology of this kind could have all sorts of implications for authentic learning techniques which attempted to connect students, graduates and academics from different places, cohorts or even eras; imagine the potential of this kind of interaction for vertically integrated projects, for example. The use of avatars could also have positive implications for the development of transferable skills and the use of reflective practice, but in all these situations, we'd urge designers to consider the extent to which environments could be co-created with students and how they may contribute to the refining or improvement of these settings over time.

Alongside the technological advances, there are more straightforward opportunities for academics to share authentic approaches across disciplines and fields of study. Some of our case study approaches have been used across institutions (placements, event management and public engagement, for example); others are ripe for experimentation (vertically integrated projects, legacy projects and curation). Increasingly, colleagues are contemplating the ways in which their approaches complement broader pedagogical skills development or assessment strategies and are innovating at the level of curriculum design. Work at the University of Liverpool, where colleagues are encouraged to prioritise 'authentic assessment', is a good example of positive, university-wide progress.

We think it likely that the benefits of authentic learning will spread more widely. This may be, in part, because we feel that authentic approaches can make a real contribution to civic engagement and to the ways in which institutions respond to national or international crisis like the Covid-19 pandemic. Our summary of international approaches in Chapter 5 provides inspiration in this context. But it's also because the academics who lead these innovations are inevitably good collaborators, happy to share in order to help others, and happy to engage in reflection and conversation to ensure that their practice continues to help students learn and thrive.

In conclusion

We hope our handbook has encouraged you to join this adventure in some way and to explore the benefits that authentic learning can offer you, your students and your partners in local communities and economies. Our case studies demonstrate that authentic learning approaches are possible in all kinds of institutions and in all types of disciplines and fields. Many of our contributors spoke of the ways in which authentic learning gave them a renewed sense of educative purpose and noted while there were many challenges to overcome, the process had been fulfilling and enlivening for them as individuals.

Of course, our participants are all advocates for the forms of learning with which they're associated. We didn't include aborted attempts in our sample and have only presented projects that have stood the tests of time and institutional change. We acknowledge this weakness in our approach and also – more generally – the limitations of our own lenses as white, middle-class, able-bodied, male higher education professionals. Authors from other backgrounds and traditions will interpret authentic learning differently and probably more effectively, but we hope that our work can act as a starting point for discussion, deliberation and doing.

In closing, we challenge you to be reflective as you explore this realm. You must know how your own personal and professional values and beliefs will shape the decisions you make about how you manage a programme. This will impact with whom you choose to work and how you choose to work with them. Embracing authentic learning will have consequences for you. It's not only a messy endeavour, there's no knowing what will happen, and the certainties and cycles that characterise much of academic life are likely to be less prominent. It may be that it will have (unintended) implications for your own (academic) identity, and, indeed, you may have to go through a process of 'unbecoming.' Ultimately, this is a field in which you're likely to have agency. You and your institution carry power and influence, and while this means that you'll be able to act and have impact, others will be affected by what you do. Throughout all of this, everyone has the opportunity to choose differently. You, your students or your partners may learn that authentic learning isn't for them. This has to be okay in order for these approaches to work. Hear others, embrace their concerns and build collaboratively, and you stand a good chance of sharing the benefits that our contributors have been so happy to celebrate and communicate.

Note

1 The Kobayashi Maru is a fictional training simulation that features in film and television's *Star Trek*. Captain James T Kirk is famously the only individual ever to have defeated the challenge.

References

Adams, J (2013) The fourth age of research. *Nature*, 497, pp 557–560

Anderson, J & Priest, C (2017) Following John Hejduk's Fabrications: On imagination and reality in the architectural design process. *Architectural Research Quarterly*, 21(2), pp 183–192. doi:10.1017/S1359135517000264

Archer, L (2008a) Younger academics' constructions of 'authenticity', 'success' and professional identity. *Studies in Higher Education*, 33(4), pp 385–403

Archer, L (2008b) The new neoliberal subjects? Young/er academics' constructions of professional identity. *Journal of Education Policy*, 23(3), pp 265–285

Barnett, R (2014) *Thinking and Rethinking the University: The Selected Works of Ronald Barnett*. London: Routledge

Barnett, R (2013) *Imagining the University*. London: Routledge

Barnett, R (2011) *Being a University*. London: Routledge

Barnett, R (1997) *Higher Education: A Critical Business*. London: Open University Press with the Society for Research into Higher Education.

Baxter Magolda, M B (1999) *Creating Contexts for Learning and Self-Authorship: Constructive-Developmental Pedagogy*. Nashville: Vanderbilt University Press

Baxter Magolda, M B (1992) Students' epistemologies and academic experiences: Implications for pedagogy. *Review of Higher Education*, 15(3), pp 265–287

Baxter Magolda, M B & Hall, M (2017) *Authoring Your Life: Developing an Internal Voice to Navigate Life's Challenges*. Sterling, VA: Sterling

Becher, T & Trowler, P (2001) *Academic Tribes and Territories* (2nd edition). Buckingham: The Open University and the Society for Research into Higher Education

Belbin, R M (1993) *Team Roles at Work*. London: Routledge

Biggs, J & Tang, C S (2011). *Teaching for Quality Learning at University: What the Student Does*. Maidenhead: McGraw-Hill

Billot, J (2010) The imagined and the real: Identifying the tensions for academic identity. *Higher Education Research & Development*, 29(6), pp 709–721

Bligh, D (2000) *What's the Use of Lectures?* London: Jossey-Bass

Bloom, B S (1956) *Taxonomy of Educational Objectives, Handbook I: The Cognitive Domain*. New York: David McKay

Boehm, C (2019) Environment trumps content: University in the knowledge society. *WonkHE*, 16 July. Available at: https://wonkhe.com/blogs/what-is-of-value-in-our-universities/?utm_medium=email&utm_campaign=Wonkhe%20Holiday%20Briefing%20-%2022%2022%20July&utm_content=Wonkhe%20Holiday%20Briefing%20-%2022%2022%20July+CID_8cdaa688a3782cbc8a34ff660d0179a0&utm_source=Email%20marketing%20software&utm_term=learning%20

content%20of%20universities%20matters%20less%20than%20the%20qual-
ity%20of%20the%20learning%20environment (Accessed: 16 September 2019)

Boschma, R (2005) Proximity and innovation: A critical assessment. *Regional Studies*, 39(1), pp 61–74. doi:10.1080/0034340052000320887

Boud, D & Solomon, N (eds) (2001) *Work Based Learning: A New Higher Education?* Buckingham: Society for Research into Higher Education

Bourner, T (2010) A compatible partnership? Student-community engagement and traditional university education. *Gateways: International Journal of Community Research and Engagement*, 3, pp 139–154

Brennan, J, Durazzi, N & Sene, T (2013) Things we know and don't know about the wider benefits of higher education: A review of the recent literature. *Department for Business, Innovation & Skills Research Paper 133*, BIS, London

Brewis, G (2014) *A Social History of Student Volunteering: Britain and Beyond, 1880–1980.* Basingstoke: Palgrave Macmillan

Burke, P J, Crozier, G & Misiaszek, L I (2017) *Changing Pedagogical Spaces in Higher Education: Diversity, Inequalities and Misrecognition.* Oxon: Routledge

Bush, K & Saltarelli, D (eds) (2000) *The Two Faces of Education in Ethnic Conflict: Towards a Peacebuilding Education for Children.* Siena: UNICEF Innocenti Research Centre

Butin, D (2010) *The Future of Community Engagement in Higher Education.* New York: Palgrave Macmillan

Centre for Social Justice and Community Action and National Co-ordinating Centre for Public Engagement (2012) *Community-Based Participatory Research: A Guide to Ethical Principles and Practices.* Bristol: NCCPE.

Clark, K (2017) Myth of the genius solitary scientist is dangerous. *The Conversation.* Available at: https://theconversation.com/myth-of-the-genius-solitary-scientist-is-dangerous-87835

Clarke, M, Hyde, A & Drennan, J (2013) Professional identity in higher education. In B M Kehm & U Teichler (eds) *The Academic Profession in Europe: New Tasks and New Challenges.* Dordrecht, Netherlands: Springer Netherlands. Pp 7–21

Colley, H, James, D & Diment, K (2007) Unbecoming teachers: Towards a more dynamic notion of professional participation. *Journal of Education Policy*, 22(2), pp 173–193

Collini, S (2012) *What Are Universities For?* London: Penguin.

Crawford, K (2012) Rethinking the student-teacher nexus: Students as consultants on teaching in higher education. In M Neary, H Stevenson & L Bell (eds) *Towards Teaching in Public: Reshaping the Modern University.* London: Continuum International Publishing. Pp 52–67

Cross, N (2011) *Design Thinking: Understanding How Designers Think and Work.* London: Berg

De Bono, E (2015) *Serious Creativity: How to Be Creative Under Pressure and Turn Ideas into Action.* London: Random House

De Bono, E (1992) *Serious Creativity: Using the Power of Lateral Thinking to Create New Ideas.* London: Harper Business

The Dearing Report (1997) *Higher Education and the Learning Society: Main Report.* London: HMSO

Deem, R, Hillyard, S & Reed, M (2007) *Knowledge, Education and New Managerialism*. Oxford: Oxford University Press

Delanty, G (2001) *Challenging Knowledge: The University in the Knowledge Society*. Buckingham: The Society for Research into Higher Education

Dewey, J (1916) *Democracy and Education*. London: Macmillan

Dweck, C (2006) *Mindset: The New Psychology of Success*. New York: Ballantine Books

Edmonson, V (2018) *The Thinking Strategist: Unleashing the Power of Strategic Management to Identify, Explore and Solve Problems*. Bingley: Emerald Publishing

Equality Challenge Unit (2009) *The Experience of Black and Minority Ethnic Staff Working in Higher Education*. London: ECU

Facer, K & Enright, B (2016) *Creating Living Knowledge, University of Bristol and AHRC Connected Communities Programme*. Bristol: University of Bristol/AHRC Connected Communities

Farrugia, C & Lane, J (2012) Legitimacy in cross-border higher education: Identifying stakeholders of international branch campuses. *Journal of Studies in International Education*, 17(4), pp 414–432

Favish, J (2009) The role of public universities: Examining one university's response to xenophobia. *Gateways: International Journal of Community Research and Engagement*, 2, pp 160–177

Fitzmaurice, M (2013) Constructing professional identity as a new academic: A moral endeavour. *Studies in Higher Education*, 38(4), pp 613–622

Fletcher, A (2019) Landscapes of communities and power. *A Paper Presented to CDJ Thinkery: Community Organising for Social Action*, London, 3 July.

Freeman, S, Eddy, S, McDonough, M, Smith, M, Okoroafor, N & Wenderoth, M (2014) Active learning increases student performance in science, engineering and mathematics. *Proceedings of the National Academy of Sciences of the United States (PNAS)*, 111(23), pp 8410–8415, 10 June. doi:10.1073/pnas.1319030111

Freire, P (2013) *Education for Critical Consciousness*. London: Bloomsbury

Freire, P (1970) *Pedagogy of the Oppressed*. New York: Herder and Herder

French, S (2015) *The Benefits and Challenges of Modular Higher Education Curricula*. Melbourne: Melbourne Centre for the Study of Higher Education

Fung, D (2017) *A Connected Curriculum for Higher Education*. London: UCL Press

Furco, A (1996) Service-learning: A balanced approach to experiential education, expanding boundaries. *Service Learning, General*, 128, pp 2–6. Available at: https://digitalcommons.unomaha.edu/slceslgen/128

Gibbons, M, Limoges, C M, Nowotny, H, Scott, P & Trow, M (1994) *The New Production of Knowledge: The Dynamics of Science and Research in Contemporary Societies*. London: Sage

Gibbs, G (1981) *Twenty Terrible Reasons for Lecturing*. SCED Occasional Paper, 8 (eBook). Birmingham.

Ginott, H (1972) *Teacher and Child: A Book for Parents and Teachers*. New York: Simon and Schuster.

Giroux, H (1988) *Teachers as Intellectuals: Towards a Critical Pedagogy of Learning*. Westport, CT: Bergin and Garvey Press

Grint, K (2010) *Leadership: A Very Short Introduction*. Oxford: Oxford University Press

Guild HE (2018) *Practice Informed Learning: The Rise of the Dual Professional.* London: Guild HE.

Haggis, T (2006) Pedagogies for diversity: Retaining critical challenge amidst fears of 'dumbing down.' *Studies in Higher Education*, 31(5), pp 521–535

Hall, B (2019) In the spirit of Gandhi ji – Thoughts on higher education. *University World News*, 26 October. Available at: www.universityworldnews.com/post. php?story=20191007113224304 (Accessed: 20 January 2020)

Hall, M (2009) Transgressive partnerships: Community engagement in a South African university. *Journal of Community Research and Engagement*, 2, pp 1–17

Harari, Y (2014) *Sapiens: A Brief History of Humankind.* London: Harvell Sector

Harriss, H. (2014) Co-authoring a live project manifesto. In H Harriss & L Widder (eds) *Architecture Live Projects: Pedagogy into Practice.* London: Routledge.

Harriss, S (2005) Rethinking academic identities in neo-liberal times. *Teaching in Higher Education*, 10(4), pp 421–433

Healey, M, Flint, A & Harrington, K (2014) *Engagement in Partnership: Students as Partners in Learning and Teaching in Higher Education.* York: The Higher Education Academy

Healey, M & Jenkins, A (2009) *Developing Undergraduate Research and Inquiry.* York: The Higher Education Academy

Henkel, M (2005) Academic identity and autonomy in a changing policy environment. *Higher Education*, 49(1), pp 155–176

Herrington, A J & Herrington, J A (2006) What is an authentic learning environment? In A J Herrington & J A Herrington (eds) *Authentic Learning Environments in Higher Education.* Hershey, PA: Information Science Publishing. Pp 1–13

Herrington, J A & Herrington, A J (1998) Authentic assessment and multimedia: How university students respond to a model of authentic assessment. *Higher Education Research and Development*, 17(3), pp 305–322

Herrington, J A & Oliver, R (2000) An instructional design framework for authentic learning environments. *Educational Technology Research and Development*, 48(3), pp 23–48

Higher Education Funding Council for Wales (2018) *Enhancing Civic Mission and Community Engagement.* Caerffili: HEFCW

Horner, L K (2016) *Co-Constructing Research: A Critical Literature Review.* Bristol: University of Bristol/AHRC Connected Communities

Hughes, J & Nicholson, H (eds) (2016) *Critical Perspectives on Applied Theatre.* Cambridge: Cambridge University Press

Huxham, C & Beech, N (2008) Inter-organizational power. In S Cropper, C Huxham, M Ebers & P Smith-Ring (eds) *The Oxford Handbook of Inter-Organisational Relations.* Oxford: Oxford University Press

Huxham, C & Vangen, S (2005) *Managing to Collaborate: The Theory and Practice of Collaborative Advantage.* Abingdon: Routledge

Institute of Student Employers (2018) *The Global Skills Gap in the C21st.* London: ISE

James, L & Cassidy, R (2018) Authentic assessment in business education: Its effects on student satisfaction and promoting behaviour. *Studies in Higher Education*, 43(3), pp 401–415. doi:10.1080/03075079.2016.1165659

Jin, L & Cortazzi, M (2006) Changing practices in Chinese cultures of learning. *Language, Culture and Curriculum*, 19(1), pp 5–20

Jongbloed, B, Enders, J & Salerno, C (2008) Higher education and its communities: Interconnections, interdependencies and a research agenda. *Higher Education*, 56, pp 303–324

Kerstetter, K (2012) Insider, outsider, or somewhere in between: The impact of researchers' identities on the community-based research process. *Journal of Rural Social Sciences*, 27(2), pp 99–117

Kezar, A & Rhoads, R (2001) The dynamic tensions of service learning in higher education: A philosophical perspective. *The Journal of Higher Education*, 72(2), pp 148–171

King's College London (2018) *Service Strategy: A Framework for Delivery*. King's College London. Available at: www.kcl.ac.uk/aboutkings/strategy/kings-service-strategy.pdf (Accessed: 13 February 2020)

Kings Fund (2020) *Our Ethical Collaboration Policy*. Kings Fund. Available at: www.kingsfund.org.uk/about-us/who-we-are/independence/ethical-collaboration (Accessed: 10 January 2020)

Klinenberg, E (2018) *Palaces for the People: How to Build a More Equal and United Society*. London: Vintage Books

Knight, P & Yorke, M (2003) Employability and good learning in higher education. *Teaching in Higher Education*, 8(1), pp 3–16

Kreber, C. (2013) *Authenticity in and Through Teaching in Higher Education: The Transformative Potential of the Scholarship of Teaching*. London: Routledge

Land, R, Rattray, J & Vivian, P (2014) Learning in the liminal space: A semiotic approach to threshold concepts. *Higher Education*, 67, pp 199–217

Lea, M & Street, B (2006) The 'academic literacies' model: Theory and applications. *Theory into Practice*, 45(4), pp 368–377

Leal, P A (2007) Participation: The ascendancy of a buzzword in the neo-liberal era. *Development in Practice*, 17(4–5), pp 539–548

Lizzio, A & Wilson, K (2013) Early intervention to support the academic recovery of first-year students at risk of non-continuation. *Innovations in Education and Teaching International*, 50(2), pp 109–120

Lounsbury, M & Pollack, S (2001) Institutionalizing civic engagement: Shifting logics and the cultural repackaging of service-learning in US higher education. *Organization*, 8(2), pp 319–339

Macfarlane, B (2010) The morphing of academic practice: Unbundling and the rise of the para-academic. *Higher Education Quarterly*, 65(1), pp 59–73

Mann, S (2008) *Study, Power and the University*. Buckingham: The Open University and The Society for Research into Higher Education

Martin, B (2012) Are universities and university research under threat? Towards an evolutionary model of university speciation. *Cambridge Journal of Economics*, 36, pp 543–565

Mason O'Connor, K, McEwen, L, Owen, D, Lynch, K & Hill, S (2011) *Embedding Community Engagement in the Curriculum*. Bristol: National Centre for Co-ordinating Public Engagement

McLean, M (2006) *Pedagogy and the University: Critical Theory and Practice*. London: Continuum

McLean, M, Abbas, A & Ashwin, P (2018) *Quality in Undergraduate Education: How Powerful Knowledge Disrupts Inequality*. London: Bloomsbury

McPherson, M, Smith-Lovin, L & Cook, J (2001) Birds of a feather: Homophily in social networks. *Annual Review of Sociology*, 27, pp 415–444

Millican, J (2017) *Universities and Conflict: The Role of Higher Education on Conflict and Resistance*. London: Routledge

Millican, J & Bourner, T (2014) *Learning to Make a Difference: Student-Community Engagement and the Higher Education Curriculum*. London: The National Voice for Lifelong Learning

Moon, J (2004) *A Handbook of Reflective and Experiential Learning*. London: Routledge

Moon, J (1999) *Reflection in Learning and Professional Development: Theory and Practice*. London: Routledge

Muhammad, M, Wallerstein, N, Sussman, A L, Avila, M, Belone, L & Duran, B (2015) Reflections on researcher identity and power: The impact of positionality on community based participatory research (CBPR) processes and outcomes. *Critical Sociology*, 41(7–8), pp 1045–1063

Naidoo, R & Jamieson, I (2006) Empowering participants or corroding learning? Towards a research agenda on the impact of student consumerism in higher education. In H Lauder, P Brown, J Dillabough & A H Halsey (eds) *Education, Globalization, and Social Change*. Oxford: Oxford University Press. Pp 875–885

Naidoo, R & Jamieson, I (2005) Empowering participants or corroding learning? Towards a research agenda on the impact of student consumerism in higher education. *Journal of Education Policy*, 20(3), pp 267–281

Naidoo, R, Shankar, A & Veer, E (2011) The consumerist turn in higher education: Policy aspirations and outcomes. *Journal of Marketing Management*, 27(11–12), pp 1142–1162

Naidoo, R & Williams, J (2015) The neoliberal regime in English higher education: Charters, consumers and the erosion of the public good. *Critical Studies in Education*, 56(2), pp 208–223

National Co-Ordinating Centre for Public Engagement (2019) *Achieving Equity in Place-Based Research, Innovation and Public Engagement*. Bristol: NCCPE

National Co-Ordinating Centre for Public Engagement & UK Community Partner Network (2016) *Principles of Practice for Community-University Partnership Working*. Bristol: NCCPE

Neary, M & Winn, J (2009) The student as producer: Reinventing the student experience in higher education. In L Bell, H Stevenson & M Neary (eds) *The Future of Higher Education: Policy, Pedagogy and the Student Experience*. London: Continuum Books

Newmann, F, King, B & Carmichael, D (2007) *Authentic Instruction and Assessment: Common Standards for Rigor and Relevance in Teaching Academic Subjects*. Des Moines, IA: Iowa Department of Education

Nichols, N, Anucha, U, Houwer, R & Wood, M (2013) Building equitable community-academic research collaborations. *Gateways: International Journal of Community Research and Engagement*, 6(1), pp 57–76

Obura, A (2003) *Never Again: Educational Reconstruction in Rwanda*. Paris: International Institute for Educational Planning

Owen, D & Hill, S (2011) *Embedding Public Engagement in the Curriculum: A Framework for the Assessment of Student Learning from Public Engagement.* Bristol: National Co-ordinating Centre for Public Engagement

Owen, D, Millican, J, Dallasheh, W & Zubeidat, I (2018) 'Us' and 'them': The role of higher education within conflict societies. In S Jackson (ed) *Developing Transformative Spaces in Higher Education: Learning to Transgress.* London: Routledge

Putman, R (2000) *Bowling Alone: The Collapse and Revival of American Community.* New York: Simon and Schuster Paperbacks

Quigley, S A (2011) Academic identity: A modern perspective. *Educate*, 11(1), pp 20–30

Race, P (2006) *The Lecturer's Toolkit.* London: Routledge

Ranson, S & Stewart, J (1998) The learning democracy. In S Ranson (ed) *Inside the Learning Society.* London: Cassell Education. Pp 253–272

Shapin, S (2012) The ivory tower: The history of a figure of speech and its cultural uses. *The British Journal for the History of Science*, 45(1), pp 1–27

Sigmon, R (1994) *Partial List of Experiential Learning Terms and Their Definitions.* Raleigh: National Society for Experiential Education

Singh, W (2018) Towards 'engaged' teaching in higher education in India. *Association of Commonwealth Universities*, 25 July. Available at: www.acu.ac.uk/news/towards-engaged-teaching-in-higher-education-in-india/ (Accessed: 28 October 2019)

Slay, H S & Smith, D A (2011) Professional identity construction: Using narrative to understand the negotiation of professional and stigmatized cultural identities. *Human Relations*, 64(1), pp 85–107

Smolovic-Jones, O & Jacklin-Jarvis, C (2016a) Week 1: Thinking about collaborative leadership. *OpenLearn Course Notes, Collaborative Leadership in Voluntary Organisations.* Milton Keynes: The Open University. Available at: www.open.edu/openlearn/money-business/collaborative-leadership-voluntary-organisations/content-section-overview?active-tab=content-tab (Accessed: 8 April 2019)

Smolovic-Jones, O & Jacklin-Jarvis, C (2016b) Week 8: Weaving the collaborative fabric. *OpenLearn Course Notes, Collaborative Leadership for Voluntary Organisations.* Milton Keynes: The Open University. Available at: www.open.edu/openlearn/money-business/collaborative-leadership-voluntary-organisations/content-section-overview?active-tab=content-tab (Accessed: 3 November 2019)

Sotiriadou, P, Logan, D, Daly, A & Guest, R (2019) The role of authentic assessment to preserve academic integrity and promote skill development and employability. *Studies in Higher Education.* doi:10.1080/03075079.2019.1582015

Stoecker, R, Tryon, E & Hilgendorf, A (2009) *The Unheard Voices: Community Organizations and Service Learning.* Philadelphia Temple University Press

Streeting, W & Wise, G (2009) *Rethinking the Values of Higher Education – Consumption, Partnership, Community?* Gloucester: Quality Assurance Agency.

Suchman, M C (1995) Managing legitimacy: Strategic and institutional approaches. *Academy of Management Review*, 20(3), pp 571–610

Tangey, S, Sutcliffe, M & Matheson, R (eds) (2018) *Transition in, Through and out of Higher Education.* London: Routledge

Thody, A (2012) Teaching in public: Revolution as evolution in nineteenth century higher education. In M Neary, H Stevenson & L Bell (eds) *Towards Teaching in Public: Reshaping the Modern University*. London: Continuum International Publishing

Tomlinson, M (2017) Student perceptions of themselves as 'consumers' of higher education. *British Journal of Sociology of Education*, 38(4), pp 450–467

The Truth and Reconciliation Commission of Canada (2015) *Honouring the Truth, Reconciling for the Future: Summary of the Final Report of the Truth and Reconciliation Commission of Canada*. Winnipeg: Truth and Reconciliation Commission of Canada

Turner, P (1987) *Campus: An American Planning Tradition*. London: MIT Press

UK Research and Innovation (2020a) *Industrial Strategy Challenge Fund*. UKRI. Available at: www.ukri.org/innovation/industrial-strategy-challenge-fund/ (Accessed: 30 January 2020)

UK Research and Innovation (2020b) *Knowledge Exchange Framework (KEF)*. UKRI. Available at: https://re.ukri.org/knowledge-exchange/knowledge-exchange-framework/ (Accessed: 30 January 2020)

UK Research and Innovation (2020c) *Strength in Places Fund*. UKRI. Available at: www.ukri.org/funding/funding-opportunities/strength-in-places-fund/ (Accessed: 30 January 2020)

UK Research and Innovation (2020d) *Public Engagement*. UKRI. Available at: www.ukri.org/public-engagement/ (Accessed: 30 January 2020)

University of Canterbury (2020) *Rebuilding Christchurch – An Introduction to Community Engagement in Tertiary Studies*. University of Canterbury. Available at: www.canterbury.ac.nz/courseinfo/GetCourseDetails.aspx?course=CHCH101&occurrence=13S2(C)&year=2013 (Accessed: 4 February 2020)

University of Cardiff (2020) *Community Gateway*. University of Cardiff. Available at: www.cardiff.ac.uk/community-gateway (Accessed: 30 January 2020)

Villarroel, V, Bloxham, S, Bruna, C & Herrera-Seda, C (2018) Authentic assessment: Creating a blueprint for course design. *Assessment & Evaluation in Higher Education*, 43(5), pp 840–854. doi:10.1080/02602938.2017.1412396

von Foerster, H. (2003) *Understanding Understanding: Essays on Cybernetics and Cognition*. New York: Springer

Watson, D, Hollister, R, Stroud, S & Babcock, E (2011) *The Engaged University: International Perspectives on Civic Engagement*. London: Routledge

Webb, S A (2015) Professional identity and social work. *A Paper Presented to 5th International Conference on Sociology & Social Work: New Directions in Critical Sociology & Social Work: Identity, Narratives and Praxis*, Glasgow Caledonian University, 26–27 August. Available at: www.chester.ac.uk/sites/files/chester/WEBB.pdf (Accessed: 9 May 2019)

World Economic Forum (2018) *The Future of Jobs Report 2018*. Geneva: World Economic Forum

Young, M & Muller, J (2013) On the powers of powerful knowledge. *Review of Education*, 1(3), pp 229–250

Index

Note: Page numbers in *italics* indicate a figure on the corresponding page. Page numbers followed by "n" indicate an endnote.